TERRY GAINER

When TRAINS RULED THE ROCKIES

My Life at the Banff Railway Station

FOREWORD BY MARCIA PILGERAM

RMB

First Edition

For information on purchasing bulk quantities of this book, or to obtain media excerpts or invite the author to speak at an event, please visit rmbooks.com and select the "Contact" tab.

RMB | Rocky Mountain Books Ltd.
rmbooks.com
@rmbooks
facebook.com/rmbooks

Cataloguing data available from Library and Archives Canada
ISBN 9781771603010 (paperback)
ISBN 9781771603034 (electronic)

Printed and bound in Canada by Friesens

We would like to also take this opportunity to acknowledge the traditional territories upon which we live and work. In Calgary, Alberta, we acknowledge the Niitsitapi (Blackfoot) and the people of the Treaty 7 region in Southern Alberta, which includes the Siksika, the Piikuni, the Kainai, the Tsuut'ina and the Stoney Nakoda First Nations, including Chiniki, Bearpaw and Wesley First Nations. The City of Calgary is also home to the Métis Nation of Alberta, Region III. In Victoria, British Columbia, we acknowledge the traditional territories of the Lkwungen (Esquimalt, and Songhees), Malahat, Pacheedaht, Scia'new, T'Sou-ke and W̱SÁNEĆ (Pauquachin, Tsartlip, Tsawout, Tseycum) peoples.

We acknowledge the financial support of the Government of Canada through the Canada Book Fund and the Canada Council for the Arts, and of the province of British Columbia through the British Columbia Arts Council and the Book Publishing Tax Credit.

Canada | Canada Council for the Arts | Conseil des arts du Canada | British Columbia | British Columbia Arts Council, An agency of the Province of British Columbia

This book is dedicated to my wonderful daughter Chantal,
without whose encouragement and support
I never would have gone the distance.
Who knew I could write anything?
It seems you did.

TABLE OF CONTENTS

Foreword *vii*
Preface *xi*
Acknowledgements *xiii*
Introduction *1*

Part I – The Golden Years: When Trains Ruled the Rockies 3

The Canadian Pacific Railway *5*
My Path to Banff: The Romance Begins *7*
To Banff on a Train in 1948 *11*
Hollywood Comes to Town *17*
The Trains to Banff: 1948 – 1954 *25*

Part II – Special Trains 39

Here Come the Royals *41*
The Grey Cup Special *49*
The Banff Springs Hotel Staff Trains *53*
The Banff Winter Carnival Special *57*
The Partners: From Station to Village to Resort *65*
Communications Central *73*

Part III – In the Train Station's Backyard 77

The Ice House and the Water Tower *143*
The Station Bush *151*
Forty Mile and Whiskey Creeks *161*
The Changing Ecosystem *167*

Part IV – The Glory Years 1955 – 1962:
I've Been Working on the Railroad... 173

Fabulous '50s *175*
Change and Innovation: A Revolution on the Rails *183*
A Summer Day at the Station *189*
Express and Freight: The Community Lifeblood *199*
The Station Orchestra: Conductors, Photographers and Concessionaires *203*
The Baggage Room *209*
Lunchtime Fishing and the Quarters Game: Strange Perks? *213*
Redcap Days: The Top of My World *217*
A Very Social Caboose *233*
Where Were You in '62? *235*

Part V – An Ending or a Beginning? 241

Moving On *243*

Epilogue *247*
About the Author *253*

FOREWORD

BY MARCIA PILGERAM

Terry Gainer loves to talk about trains. After a 20-year-long friendship, I'm not surprised that we met over train talk when he simply cold-called me to do just that. At the time, I was the CEO of a small private rail company, and Terry – curious as always – wanted to talk about trains, specifically the one I was operating from Sandpoint, Idaho, to Livingston, Montana. He wanted to know exactly where we went, what kind of equipment we operated and all the other details. When you run a company, you take a lot of phone calls, but that call stuck out in my mind, and, after a while, I found myself looking forward to his increasingly frequent (and inquisitive) calls.

It wouldn't be long before he was working with me. We collaborated over new tour routes, equipment and industry markets. Terry is a quintessential salesman: he's talkative, friendly and extremely knowledgeable. While a business venture originally brought us together, it's a deeply rooted friendship that has kept us together over the course of many years. We both were single parents with daughters of similar age (and the fact we both have Irish blood and the gift of gab weaved into our DNA didn't hurt either). We both love to share a story or two, over a drink or two. But what we really had in common was our lifelong love of trains. I've yet to meet another individual who remembers more about a train – its route and schedule, the exact cars in the consist (and their layout) and, undoubtedly, the name of the conductor he'd met 40 years ago – than my pal, Terry. His extraordinary memory and recall is evident throughout every chapter of this book. His memory is like an old file cabinet, brimming with fascinating details of every train he's ever encountered and every person he's ever met.

I have never tired of his stories and had myriad opportunities to hear them as we often criss-crossed the country by plane, train and automobile to meet and collaborate with other train operators, cruise lines, travel agents and the occasional recruits for our growing team. Once, we had a chance to deadhead (reposition) a railcar recently purchased by our company from Chicago to Seattle, and we were positioned as the last car on Amtrak's Westbound Empire Builder. For whatever reason, we thought it would be a grand idea to bring along a potential sales hire, ensuring we'd have some real quality time for a final interview with this promising candidate. We met at Union Station in Chicago and boarded the newly purchased crew sleeper/baggage car to begin our westward trip.

I'd brought along two days of supplies to nourish us along the route, but it turned out that the train line power had not been connected to our car. Thus, there would be no cooking and no lights, and worse, no air conditioning for our August journey. We left the baggage door ajar and sat on makeshift seats of metal crates and wooden boxes. Though I'd heard many of the train tales of Banff more than once, he told them so well that I always looked forward to hearing them again and again on that trip. We spent two captive days, regaled to the point of tears, with yet more tales of his youthful (mis)adventures. On the rare occasion when the train station stop was long enough, I'd hop off for some real food to share on our baggage-car adventure.

And, in the cool of the dark evenings, long after our potential job candidate found his way to his sleeping berth, Terry and I passed many an hour in the baggage compartment, below the starlit sky, pondering the sad demise of real passenger rail service. I will long remember that trip (and the candidate, who not surprisingly, declined our job offer).

Terry has covered thousands of miles by train, and, besides our infamous baggage-car journey, I was lucky enough to have shared many other rail miles with him, perched high in a vintage streamliner dome car, taking in the panoramic views of the Rocky Mountains, where he'd arguably win the debate of whose range of the Rockies was more spectacular. I had to concede: we'll always agree that nothing compares to his Canadian Rockies (though there's a lot we still argue over to this day). Even now, I can almost hear the thundering roar of the crowd at the Banff station, and the awe of young Terry, as the sleek Canadian glided into the Banff station for the first time. Terry's stories transport me to the halcyon days of Banff and the great trains filled with tourists, eager to explore the grand Canadian Rockies.

Over the course of 20 years, I've had the good fortune to visit his childhood land of legends and lore and anecdotes, and I've even walked a bit of the trail that leads deep into the woods and the den of the notorious Station Bush Gang. It's not far from the Banff train station, where Terry came of age, in the streamliner age of rail travel. Over the course of his lifetime, he watched first-hand as the old workhorse steam engines were replaced with sleek new diesel locomotives, and dozens of trains rolled through Banff and her iconic mountains, providing unlimited opportunities for Terry and his band of buddies. I've met some of these boys and girls from Banff, and I marvel at how the bonds of friendship, cultivated a half-century ago, are still strong to this day.

From a small boy in a polished suit, travelling by train alongside his parents, to the young man who stood overhead the Banff train station to watch the arrival of the future queen of England on her Royal Train, Terry's stories will fascinate you. You'll be entertained by the escapades of this self-assured young man who donned the infamous redcap to manhood and then, with a pocketful of summer savings, headed halfway around the world. More than 50 years later, his wanderlust continues, and I frequently bid him farewell as he heads off on yet another adventure. But his heart is deeply rooted in his beloved "Banff the Beautiful," and he's never forgotten about his lifelong friends, "The Boys and Girls from Banff." And after you've read the recollections of this adventurous young man, from a simple mountain village, I suspect you won't either.

PREFACE

When Trains Ruled the Rockies is a history of the Banff train station and the surrounding community during the period 1948 through 1962. I draw on the memories and experiences from those halcyon years when I lived and worked at the CPR (Canadian Pacific Railway) station, as well as archival information and photos.

I decided to take on this project after visiting the station in the summer of 2015 to view the renovations begun by the new leaseholder. Their intent was to restore the station as close as possible to its original design. While impressed by the refurbishments and a display of original photographs adorning the walls, I was left with a hollow feeling. There was no story or evidence portraying the major role the railway and the station played in the community during the heyday of train travel. The station was the hub of the community and the largest year-round employer. Everything that arrived in Banff, including the tourists, foodstuffs and merchandise, came off the trains and through the station doors.

This book documents life at the station, the trains that came to Banff and the huge role the station played within the community. The evolving changes to life and landscape documented in the text and photos also reflect a period of rapid change in Canada generally. My own story of growing up at the station winds a thread through the narrative. Our arrival in Banff marked the beginning of my lifelong passion for passenger trains, at one time the most dominant means of transportation for Canadians but sadly fading into history. As my editor, Joan Dixon, noted, "This story is a lovely and informative requiem." With the history of passenger rail travel in Banff relatively undocumented, it needed to be brought to life by a witness and participant, and added to the bookshelf.

ACKNOWLEDGEMENTS

As I completed the last chapters of this book, I began to realize how many people guided me though this project. It also occurred to me that the acknowledgments might be the longest section in the book because I'm indebted to so many.

My thanks begin with family. In the summer of 2014, I was describing my recent visit to the Banff station to my daughter Chantal. A refurbishment was underway and it was heartwarming to see the station finally getting a facelift, but I felt something was missing, that historic photographs alone would not tell the station story. I ventured the opinion, "Maybe there needs to be a book or something." Chantal never beats around the bush, short and sweet and to the point, and said, "Dad you lived there, maybe you should write it." Chantal, you gave me the final push and I started writing. Love you and thanks.

I connected with my sisters Sylvia and Frances and brother Fred, outlining the project. They are a few years ahead of me and their recollections of our move to Banff were much more vivid than mine. I doubt I could have provided the same accuracy and detail of our early years in Banff without their input. My brother Fred immediately began to provide me with anecdotes and recollections of life at the station, providing the photographs to back it up. During his school days, his hobby was photography and many of the images in the book he not only shot but also developed. Fred was the best "big brother," breaking ground for me when we were kids, and here he was, 60 years later, helping me again. To my nephews Mark and Pat, I'm not sure what I would have done without your generosity, allowing me to "bunk in" at your respective dwellings for weeks at a time while I was researching the subject matter at the Glenbow Museum in Calgary and the Whyte Museum of the Canadian Rockies in Banff. Frankly, I could not have written this without the support of my family.

Jim Alexander and I have been friends since the mid-1950s, working together at the station and fishing every worthwhile fishing hole around Banff. Now, as then, Jim has been an excellent source of information and I've hounded him repeatedly for the last two years. His recollections and clarification of subject matter were key in maintaining the accuracy I have tried to present about life at the station. Jim's remarkable memory, and his recall of our days in Banff, is astonishing. Additionally, Jim provided me with the photos and information about his mother, Helen, who played for the famous Edmonton Grads. Jim, thank you for being my friend.

David Fleming is another "Banffite" who came to my assistance when I was floundering with my photo collection for the book. David is years younger than me, and I only knew him years ago as the son of his dad, Dr. Ray Fleming. But I met David during Back to Banff Days in June of 2017 and briefly discussed my book, mentioning I'd be using a number of black and white photographs from a family collection. David casually mentioned it was a sideline for him to find old photos for his Facebook site, Encyclopedia of Banff. He graciously worked his magic, finding images from 50 and 60 years ago that I desperately needed to provide the historical integrity for the storyline that only photographs can provide. Thank you, David, for your kind assistance and generosity.

To maintain historical accuracy and integrity, I spent hours researching train timetables, consists, seasonality and the role of other major players in the Rockies. The Whyte Museum and Archives of the Canadian Rockies in Banff, Alberta, and the Glenbow Museum in Calgary, Alberta, provided me with many confirmations, including historical facts, timelines and photographs. As an unexpected bonus, my research unearthed valuable information I had either forgotten or been unaware of, thus enriching the project. Both facilities are outstanding and their staff members went well beyond the call of duty to guide me. I especially want to thank Lena Goon, who has been the "rock" at Archives of the Canadian Rockies for years. Without Lena's help and patience, I would have floundered badly trying to keep to my timeline. When Lena retired in 2017, Elizabeth Kundert-Cameron, head librarian and manager of reference service, must have noticed my uncertainty referencing information and immediately stepped into the breech, getting me back on track. Elizabeth then guided me through the "Use Fee Permissions and Conditions for Release of Reproductions" process and introduced me to Lindsay Stokalko, my other guiding light, who joined the archives team in 2017. Lindsay became my go-to person as I worked to finish the project in the summer of 2018. Elizabeth and Lindsay, thank you so much for your amazing support and assistance.

I am also deeply indebted to the publisher of *We Live in a Postcard, Banff Family Histories* and the Banff History Book Committee volunteers. The members of the committee donated countless hours collecting information for that excellent publication dedicated to detailing historic Banff families. This information was the icing on the cake that I could not have found elsewhere. Thank you all so much.

Steve Boyko was my first contact when I began researching

the book, struggling to find timetables and schedule information. I stumbled upon Steve's website and he responded immediately, providing me with CPR timetables from 1948 through 1952. Steve, this information was so valuable to my timeline and gave me the starting point for my project. Your encouragement along the way has been a beacon. Take time to visit Steve's website (www.traingeek.ca). I'm forever grateful I did!

I really hit the wall when I was seeking information on telegraph equipment and the systems employed in the heyday of this technology. I was getting a bit frantic and spent hours one evening surfing the internet. Somehow, I managed to connect with Harold Kramer via his website. Harold operates Amateur Radio Station WJ1B in Cheshire, Connecticut, and is a fountain of knowledge about communications technology. Harold is a true gentleman and freely accommodated my requests for images of telegraph keys, telegraph sounders and technical information. I've never had the pleasure of meeting Harold, but his cooperation and generosity is deeply appreciated. If you have an interest in telegraphy, visit his website (www.wj1b.com).

I want to thank my friend Eric Pelham, who led me to meet with Adam and Jan Waterous, whose company Liricon Capital has purchased the lease on the CPR station in Banff and the surrounding lands. Adam and Jan immediately embraced my book project, creating a display of my section, "The Ice House and the Water Tower," on a highly visible fence on the station grounds and offering their support for my book launch at the station, my first home in Banff. At a press conference in April 2017, Adam and Jan announced their plans for the redevelopment of the station and surrounding lands, including a 900-stall parking lot to ease Banff's parking crisis, plus a Railway Historic District featuring the original ice house as the centrepiece. Eric, Adam and Jan, your support and enthusiasm was a tremendous boost for me at a time when I needed the encouragement to finish the book. I thank you from my heart, not only for supporting me but for saving my favourite place in the world.

I first met Darryl Raymaker in 1960 at the University of Alberta but lost touch for a few years. We reconnected a couple of years ago and over lunch Darryl revealed he was writing a book, which was published in 2017. Darryl swears his book would still be unpublished without his editor, Joan Dixon. Darryl referred me to Joan, who accepted the challenge of working with me. Darryl, thanks for your introduction.

Joan is a miracle worker, an amazing editor and a wonderful instructor. After she schooled me on grammar and punctuation, Joan guided me through my maze of hieroglyphics to create a manuscript that brought me to the doorstep of the publisher. Joan, I am forever indebted and thank you for your insights and understanding.

As usual, my friend Marcia Pilgeram gets to have the last word. Between 1999 and 2005, Marcia was president and CEO of Montana Rockies Rail Tours, headquartered in Sandpoint, Idaho. Marcia made the dubious decision to hire me, first as a consultant on a six-month contract, which turned into five years, only threatening to throttle me a few times. Our friendship has strengthened over the years and embraces our families as well. The decision to request someone to write the foreword was a no-brainer. Thank you, Marcia, for being such a good friend and pal.

Sometime during the writing process, it occurred to me I should posthumously acknowledge the builders of the railway, without whom my future on this planet would have been in grave doubt. So thank you CPR for hiring my father – it provided him the opportunity to meet my mother, facilitating my arrival on the planet.

INTRODUCTION

In the summer of 1948, our family moved to Banff. CPR had appointed my dad, F.L. (Frank) Gainer, station agent and the position included a two-bedroom residence on top of the train station. Living only feet above the platform and main line, I could almost reach out and touch the trains, so I spent hours watching passengers step off the sleeping cars that stopped directly below. This marked the beginning of my lifelong passion for passenger trains, at one time the most dominant means of transportation for Canadians. As passenger service disappeared throughout the late '60s and '70s, the Banff train station began a slow deterioration, and the decline accelerated with the cancellation of VIA Rail's Canadian through Banff in 1990.

But, in 2012, a saviour in the form of the Banff Lodging Company leased the train station building from CPR and began a million-dollar restoration project. By the summer of 2014, this historic landmark had been tastefully refurbished in keeping with the original design of the building. That summer I toured the newly renovated station that was once my home but felt something was missing. Other than a few photographs on the interior walls and tables, little information documented the dominant role played by the Banff station during the peak years of rail travel after the Second World War through to 1962. It was not only the main transportation hub for Banff but also the hub for everything that was required to maintain the town infrastructure, including tourists, foodstuffs and merchandise.

The story needs telling; the "station" had served as the airport of the day for Banff and the surrounding communities in the Canadian Rockies. It was the bus depot, the local taxi stand, the express office, the freight office and the telecommunications centre. In fact, the Banff station was a complete community of its own. It is important to bring back the memory of those who contributed so much to "Banff the Beautiful." The gap I perceive in the history of the community spurred me to begin this project.

This is not another book detailing the history of Canada via the construction of the "National Dream," the coast-to-coast railway. Nor is it a train buff's handbook detailing technical facts about locomotives, rolling stock and railway procedures. Most of this story comes from first-hand knowledge and personal experiences, largely gained through living on top of the station with my family and working seven consecutive summers, first in the baggage room and then as a redcap.

Living at the train station helped shaped the life of this small-town boy. The revolving cast of characters I met in the late '50s and early '60s, and working the summer jobs made possible by CPR, had a huge influence on my future. In a way, this book represents my own trilogy: my love of railroads, my life as a Banff railway brat sparking my interest in travel, and the lifelong friendships of "The Boys and Girls from Banff."

PART I

The Golden Years: When Trains Ruled the Rockies

THE CANADIAN PACIFIC RAILWAY

Gordon Lightfoot's classic song "Canadian Railroad Trilogy" would make an excellent national anthem because it describes the most formative event in Canadian history. Confederation made the promise to build a transcontinental rail line west to the Pacific, guaranteeing British Columbia's participation in a new "Canada," and creating a nation that spanned the continent from coast to coast to coast.

Experts of the day scoffed at such a broad undertaking, but in 19 years the impossibility became reality. Canada's borders were set and Siding 29, the forerunner to Banff, was established in 1883. In 1886, the Canadian Pacific Railway syndicate co-founder Donald Smith and renowned railroad builder William Cornelius Van Horne drove the last spike at Craigellachie in British Columbia.

Van Horne was a man of vision and, among his many railway exploits, he led infant Canada into the world of tourism. Recognizing the spectacular scenery along the rail line as a huge international drawing card augmenting business travel, he envisioned a series of world-class hotels across the country, all connected by the luxurious passenger trains of the Canadian Pacific Railway. Van Horne famously stated, "If we can't export the scenery, we'll import the tourists." Choosing a site near Siding 29 and overlooking the Bow Falls, he commissioned the construction of the Banff Springs Hotel. Canadian Pacific Railway was Canada's first tourism marketer and continued as such well into the 20th century.

MY PATH TO BANFF: THE ROMANCE BEGINS

The day my folks announced that we were moving Banff I was only 6 years old, probably too young to realize the full significance of this decision on my future. But I do remember how the entire family greeted the announcement with joy.

The Gainer family was a railway family. Born to Irish immigrant parents in Arthur, Ontario, in 1888, Dad had been the youngest of 11 children. He struck out on his own in 1905 when he was 17, travelling to Butte, Montana, where two elder brothers worked in the copper mines. Shortly after arriving, he decided that working in a mine for 12 hours a day and boozing for another six wasn't the life he wanted, so he headed back to Canada. Dad then found work in Daysland, near Leduc, Alberta, as a freight clerk with CPR, beginning a 48-year career with Canadian Pacific.

Realizing that any sense of job security with the railway would require more qualifications, he borrowed a telegraph key to practise Morse code and in 1911 wrote the telegrapher's exams, including the rules and regulations of CPR, to qualify as an operator. Passing the exams, Dad was appointed relief agent on the Strathcona Subdivision near Edmonton. In 1911, Dad was assigned to Cochrane, Alberta, as an operator and the following year appointed agent, becoming the youngest permanent agent on the entire CPR system.

My mother, Enid Maggs, had been born in Swansea, Wales, but her family immigrated to Canada in 1911 when she was

12 years of age. Dad met the Maggs family on the day they arrived in Cochrane after the long voyage from Wales and the seven-day train journey from Halifax. Cochrane was meant to be a stopover, but Mom's father, Frederick Maggs, seemed to like the tiny community and bought the General Store (now famous as MacKay's Ice Cream). Mom became one of the first women to work in a bank in Alberta and married my father in 1922. Of the five children to follow, I was last in the line, born in May 1942. In the first half of the 20th century, the railways employed almost a quarter of Canada's working population during the golden age of steam and passenger trains. I am forever grateful I was a member of one of those families.

In 1947, Dad had been transferred from Cochrane to Lethbridge, Alberta. While on paper this may have been a significant promotion, post-war Lethbridge was not for our family. Almost on arrival, Mom was afflicted with severe hay fever, there was mud everywhere – a result of the frantic residential building spree following the war – and it seemed the wind would never quit blowing. As soon as possible, Dad bid on an upcoming position as the CP station agent in Banff.

Dad's position as Banff station agent included company housing and for the next eight years we lived in the west end residence above the current train station, which had two large balconies. The trackside balcony provided the best view in town, only feet above the detraining passengers. The townside balcony overlooked the arrivals entrance, up Lynx Street toward the town. At that time, there was no Elk Street down to Banff Avenue; the so-called station bush (the surrounding undeveloped land) extended to Squirrel Street and east to Cougar Street, plus the area west of Lynx Street to Echo Creek and the Bow River, including what is now the RCMP barracks, the Brewster Head Office and the Banff Hospital. There were no houses or buildings then, just bush. Hidden in the bush, on the site of the current RCMP barracks, was the CPR dump, where the station's refuse was deposited and burned. The dump had its own tenants; at any time of day you could spot half a dozen black bears prowling for breakfast, lunch and dinner. To a young boy, this sounded like paradise.

TO BANFF ON A TRAIN IN 1948

On Saturday, July 24, 1948, my mom, my sister Frances and I travelled to Banff from Calgary on the Dominion. As the train approached the station, I bolted from my seat. I could barely wait for the conductor to lower the steps to the platform. After weeks of excitement and speculation about our move, our family would be back together again at our new home. From the open window of the vestibule I spotted Dad and Fred waiting on the platform. They had left Lethbridge for Banff a couple of weeks prior to the rest of the family while we awaited the completion of the refurbishment after the previous agent, "Mac" McKinnon, moved out. Cecil Walker and Bill Timinsky were also there to greet us. They were station employees who worked with Dad, covering the round-the-clock shifts as telegraphers and dispatching train orders to the passenger and freight train engineers. They were to become a big part of my life.

While my mom and my sister Frances began to unpack the china barrel and immediately set up the house, Fred and I took the opportunity to disappear down the stairs and into the station. Ten-year-old Fred had already scoped out the premises, but together we scoured every nook and cranny, from the waiting room to the basement furnace room, ending up across the street at the CPR dump. There, Fred introduced me to Victor Sugg, a CP employee who was everything from gardener to maintenance man. He also appeared to be the unofficial "bear trainer." With half a dozen bears in attendance, Vic was happy to have his charges put on a bit of a show for me.

My second day in Banff was even better. After wolfing down breakfast, I tore off down the stairs and out the door. Leaning against the sandstone ledge beside the express room stood a kid about my age. He said something like, "My-name-is-Johnny-Stuckert, I-met-your-brother-last-week. A-bunch-of-us-are-going-to-play-at-the-tire-swing, wannacome?" Tire swing? I had no idea what that meant, but I wanted to go and off we went. That day I was to meet half a dozen more kids my age, including Mervin Woodworth, Billy Mackenzie and Garry McCullough, who, with Johnny, were to become my best friends during my school years.

But that tire swing! I'd never seen anything like it. Located back in the trees near Squirrel Street was an oblong depression, as if a 50-foot egg had been scooped out of the ground. A truck tire, suspended by a long, thick rope, hung down from a huge pine tree and the tire could swing through the depression about three feet off the ground. By pulling on another rope, also attached to the tire, we'd pull the tire up the hill to the edge of the crater, climb on and let go! The swing would arc through the full length of the depression and then gravity would pull it back. All day long we'd take turns on the swing, each daring to be bolder than the preceding riders, imagining ourselves as Tarzan of the mountains.

The very next spring, the tire swing would disappear, dismantled by the "government" – our local catch-all title for Parks Canada. That year, the Squirrel Street bush would also disappear, trees logged and construction begun, pushing Elk Street through to the station. It was an omen I didn't recognize at the time. The Squirrel Street bush would soon be logged, big holes dug for basements and more changes loomed ahead.

But before all that came our first Christmas in Banff – and

my most memorable. Just prior to Christmas, I had looked in the big display window at Standish Hardware only to stop dead. There it was, the stuff of my dreams, an American Flyer electric train. It had a cast iron steam locomotive and four streamlined passenger cars with New York Central Railroad markings. My eyes must have been the size of saucers. The train was to be raffled off by the Kinsmen Club at the community Christmas concert and tickets were on sale for only a dollar, but that was a big problem. I'd never had a dollar in my life; one might as well have been a million.

That evening at dinner, I wiggled the conversation around to the electric train at Standish Hardware, implying that a raffle ticket for a dollar was a good deal because they would only sell 200 tickets and I'd surely win. Dad just chuckled, reminding me that the odds were not really that great. For the next couple of weeks, I kept bugging my parents about the train raffle, but to no avail.

Then, on the evening of the concert, as we were leaving for the school auditorium, Dad handed me a raffle ticket and said, "I hope you win because this dollar came out of your Christmas present money." The ticket was number 71 and I held it in my hand through the entire evening, looking at it constantly and silently mouthing "please pick 71, please pick 71..."

The raffle was the last item on the program and it felt like a lifetime before the draw. Finally, Bus Rivett, president of the Kinsmen Club, drew a ticket and announced, "The winning ticket number is 71, Terry Gainer." Frozen to my chair, I couldn't believe my ears. Dad, equally stunned, finally said, "You'd better get up to the stage before they give it to someone else." I shot up there, tears of joy streaming down, and hugged that box containing my train set with all my might. I choked out a thank you – and to the amusement of the crowd – called out to brother Fred for help.

For the next few days, the train never left my sight. I set it up in the bedroom and played with it constantly. On Christmas morning, Dad called me to come into the living room to join the family to open the presents. After ignoring him two or three times (after all, I had what I wanted), he came stomping into my bedroom, pulled the transformer plug out of the wall and said, "Get out there right now, Mister, or I'll get rid of that train!" When Dad called you "Mister," he meant business. Out to the Christmas tree I went.

The following spring, my train world expanded when the pipeline came to town and the station's coal-burning furnace was converted to natural gas. The furnace room was directly below our residence and had a connecting staircase. As soon as the Bridge and Building Gang had cleaned out the coal and dust, Fred wasted little time in claiming the domain as his own. He was the handyman of our family and he could build and fix anything. (Dad and I, on the other hand, were a danger to society when around tools.) So Fred took it upon himself to build a model railroad for us. As he recalled years later:

> The large area where I built the table for the train had been the coal storage room. After I got permission to use the space, I did a lot more sweeping and cleaning, bought the lumber for the framework at Unwin's Lumberyard and carried it by hand back to the basement. I scrounged some plywood from around the station, using this as the tabletop. I built a wooden frame for the mountain and covered it with soaking wet burlap, allowing me to shape the mountain to my specifications.

> I laid the tracks and, then, using plaster of Paris, I covered over the burlap and, when the plaster set, I cut the tunnel entrances. After the plaster of Paris dried, I painted the mountain with various shades of green and grey paint. It all looked very real.
>
> The train could then enter the tunnel, following the tracks through to the other end. I had a Lionel train engine with two freight cars and a caboose....As your train was also 027 gauge, it fit on the same tracks. In subsequent years I added two switches (Christmas gifts from Mom and Dad), allowing me to add more track. Later I figured out a way to have operational block signals, which would light up as the train approached the station and automatically shut off when the train passed by. I had a lot of fun doing this. I learned a lot about electricity and wiring in the process.

Fred and I spent hours in the furnace room playing "railway," especially on cold winter evenings. It was our very own railway to operate and we created a station community of our own.

HOLLYWOOD COMES TO TOWN

In late July of 1948, another kind of excitement was in the air. A Hollywood production team was coming to town to shoot a movie starring a famous cowboy actor. My sister Frances was our Hollywood expert; she was even a member of a movie star fan club. Just after the arrival of the afternoon Dominion, Fran came running up the stairs to announce, "I saw him. He's here. He just got off the train and now he is by the Brewster Kiosk!" "He" was Randolph Scott, one of America's most famous cowboy heroes. Out the door we all scrambled, only to see a deluxe Brewster limousine driving away from the station, heading for the Banff Springs Hotel. Would our world ever be the same?

About the same time, CPR crews, carpenters and labourers were hard at work building something about a half-mile east of the station at the "wye," and the area had been posted off limits to the public. The wye were two tracks forming, of course, a *Y*-shape, with the top end of the *Y* joined to the main line by a set of switches. (A much more economical solution than constructing a mechanized turntable, a wye was used for turning locomotives and cars around. The locomotive would enter one branch of the *Y* that was at a 90-degree angle off the main line and proceed to the top of the straight tracks. When the locomotive cleared the *Y* junction, the brakeman would throw the switch and the locomotive would back out the other side of the *Y* facing the opposite direction.) The tracks for the north end of the Banff wye extended for about 500 yards, providing plenty of space to construct the movie set, a mock-up of a railway construction village.

The news flashed through the community like wildfire. This must be the movie set for the filming of *Canadian Pacific*, starring Randolph Scott! Mervin and I set off down the tracks to the wye to investigate. Our first attempt to visit the movie set was rebuffed by a CPR policeman who shooed us off, I guess as a safety precaution. But little did he realize he had come up against the future Station Bush Gang!

After being chased off the set, Mervin and I backtracked and then set off through the bush. Crossing Whiskey Creek and tromping through the forest, we followed a branch of Forty Mile Creek that flowed past the top end of the wye. No cops or security guys were to be seen, and we spent a good part of the morning watching the crews constructing false-front buildings and fashioning a railway camp. Also onsite was a flume-stack locomotive, an old business car and a wood-sided passenger car – no doubt donated by CPR to add period authenticity to the set.

Over the next few days, we'd wander back to the wye to spy on the filming, but nothing much ever seemed to happen. Instead of those breathtaking, broad action scenes we'd viewed in the theatres, the only filming we could see appeared to be short 20- or 30-second takes of our hero boarding a railcar, people talking or the construction crews laying down a rail. It was just plain boring. We 6-year-old critics had seen enough! There was far more action in the bush. During my school years, numerous Hollywood movies filmed in and around Banff, including *Fort Saskatchewan* with Alan Ladd and Shelly Winters, and *River of No Return* with Marilyn Monroe and Robert Mitchum. But none of them included trains or the station so I showed little interest.

Later I would watch *Canadian Pacific* mostly out of nostalgia, because the movie itself was forgettable – just another western and Hollywood perversion of history. Randolph Scott was there to save the railway from the usual villains, this time the fur trappers who incited the Indians into attacking the train. The movie's redeeming feature was the scenery. Filmed in Cinecolor, it featured spectacular vistas of the Canadian Rockies, which I didn't realize at the time was a huge marketing coup for CPR. Westerns were the genre of the day and Randolph Scott was hugely popular. It was a perfect scenario to have a Canadian Pacific/Canadian Rockies travelogue displayed in movie theatres all over the United States when you have a summer train from Chicago to get you to the Banff Springs Hotel, where Mr. Scott and the cast spent most of August. It was no coincidence the Hollywood press was in attendance, churning out all kinds of newsprint about the fabulous "Castle in the Rockies." I would later witness Canadian Pacific repeat the mastery of its Hollywood connections again and again, reinforcing the majesty of the Canadian Rockies on screen, broadcasting them to the entire world.

Travel to Banff after the Second World War had simply exploded and it all came by train – to my very great delight living above the station. The Trans-Canada Highway was still a distant dream then, so the drive from Banff to Vancouver took three or four days, an ordeal few would consider. Highway 93 south to Radium and Cranbrook on rough gravel took you to paved roads in the United States. From Spokane, Washington, you followed old Highway 2 to Seattle and then up to Vancouver. The Big Bend Highway from Golden to Revelstoke in BC closed in the early 1950s as the Mica Creek Dam project on the Columbia River flooded the roadbed. Besides, that stretch of road was hazardous, open only in the summer months and was never for the faint at heart. The trains truly ruled the Rockies.

In the 1940s through to the early 1960s, you could take a train to almost anywhere in Canada. If Canadian Pacific didn't have a train to your desired destination, Canadian National, Canada's other transcontinental railway, probably did. Branch line services feeding the main line had connecting schedules, providing seamless travel. For instance, three daily services were available from Edmonton to Calgary, all connected to a main line transcontinental train. The Edmonton/Calgary Express stopped only in Red Deer, covering the 190 miles in three hours.

Canadian Pacific also operated a second passenger service at that time through the Canadian Rockies beginning in Medicine Hat, Alberta, called the Kootenay Express, passing through the Rockies via the Crow's Nest Pass, along the shore of Kootenay Lake to Nelson, Castlegar, Penticton, Princeton and then through the Coquihalla Pass to Vancouver. The eastbound counterpart from Vancouver back to Medicine Hat was called the Kettle Valley Express. Both trains connected to the transcontinental Dominion in Medicine Hat, offering service to and from eastern Canada. In addition, trains from Medicine Hat to and from Nelson served the Kootenays with Calgary connections at Fort Macleod. There were trains going everywhere all across Canada.

For me, at least, train journeys could become unscheduled adventures. As a kid, I used to go from Banff to Rocky Mountain House most summers to visit my older sister and her husband. I got to travel on three very different trains. I'd leave Banff on Train 2 at 10:10 a.m., arriving in Calgary shortly after noon, and board the Edmonton Express on an adjacent track departing at 1:00 p.m. The Edmonton Express had first- and second-class coaches but no sleeping or dining cars. An on-board newsie sold sandwiches, newspapers and beverages, and the train averaged a speed of over 60 miles per hour. A 2:30 p.m. arrival in Red Deer allowed time to transfer to the "mixed" train for Rocky at 3:00 p.m., supposedly arriving in Rocky at 6:30 p.m. It was never on time and very basic transportation – as a local freight train with a passenger car hooked onto the tail end. With freight cars having no steam heat connections, the trainmen fired up a coal and wood pot-bellied stove at one end of the passenger car on chilly days.

In the late '40s and early '50s, the road from Red Deer to Rocky Mountain House was best described as a bog, so many folks opted for the train ride. The mixed trains were slow: Red Deer to Rocky, only 50 miles, took over three hours. At every siding and station, the mail, foodstuffs and merchandise were unloaded, freight cars shunted off the train and often livestock, bound for the packing plants, were loaded into the livestock cars.

On one most memorable trip, my friend Jimmy Christou accompanied me to Rocky. Our moms had dressed us in our best flannel slacks, white shirts and blue blazers (yes, we dressed for travel) and off we went with a food hamper large enough to feed an army. Shortly after we left Red Deer, the train stopped at Sylvan Lake and, after loading and unloading, the train crew, including the engineer, all retired to the passenger car for a coffee break. We still had a ton of food left over, so we invited the crew to help themselves. Sandwiches, cold fried chicken, cookies, baklava from Jimmy's mom: it all disappeared in minutes. After this unscheduled lunch stop, we departed Sylvan 20 minutes late but now with new best friends. The next stop was Benalto, where the crew was to load a stock car with pigs.

We were late, so the pig farmer was waiting at the loading dock and in some hurry to load quickly and depart. But Murphy's Law came into play and during the loading process one very excited pig knocked over the railing on the loading ramp and scampered back into the holding pen. Of course, the rest of the pigs bolted and followed. The holding pen was fenced, so the pigs were enclosed but none too eager to go back up the ramp. One by one, the farmer and the train crew were literally dragging the pigs into the railcar. As Jimmy and I now felt a kinship with the crew, we jumped into the fray, helping to herd the pigs around the enclosure to the loading ramp. Finally, all the pigs were loaded, and we departed Benalto an hour late.

We arrived in Rocky about 7:30 p.m. My brother-in-law was waiting for us at the station with his pickup truck, and when he saw and smelled us, he said, "Into the box, you're not sitting in the cab covered in mud and smelling like pigs!" And that was also the happy demise of my grey slacks and blue blazer. The smell just wouldn't go away.

Throughout my first summer in Banff, many days were spent just hanging out at the station. I'd spend hours on the platform watching the switch crew in action as they added or deleted passenger cars to the train consists. In between trains, my favourite spot to hang out was in the baggage room with Merle Sundberg, the baggage master. Merle was the kindest and most patient man, and it was in his baggage room that my education really began about the trains of North America. A huge map was mounted on the office wall, charting the CPR and CNR (Canadian National Railway) passenger systems across Canada, as well as the connecting rail services into the United States. There were train lines everywhere, criss-crossing the continent. Merle patiently answered my gazillion questions and took me step by step through the CP and CN train schedules that were thick as a book. Because Banff was located on the main line and a premier tourism destination, all transcontinental trains had scheduled stops here. The station was the busiest place in town, with eight passenger train arrivals daily in winter and ten per day during the summer.

THE TRAINS TO BANFF: 1948 - 1954

A good question might be, "Why all the trains to Banff?" In fact, for nine months of the year, Banff was not actually a major stop or destination and most travellers were merely "through" passengers on their way westbound to Vancouver or eastbound to Calgary, Winnipeg, Toronto and Montreal. In the 1940s and 1950s, trains were still the dominant means of transportation across the country and offered frequent daily departures. Air travel had yet to impact train travel and was considered expensive, mostly patronized by corporate travellers, politicians and executives. Until the advent of jet travel, the public also harboured safety concerns: piston-driven aircraft were unable to fly above 20,000 feet and at lower elevations the ride could be rough and very scary.

But, during the summer months, Banff was the featured destination for most tourists travelling across Canada. In addition to the year-round regularly scheduled trains, a purely tourist train called the Mountaineer operated from early June through Labour Day, transporting visitors to Banff through the Canadian Rockies to Vancouver.

The passenger trains each had their own character and catered to specific customer requirements. Even the physical makeup of the train consists (pronounced *con*-sists, with the emphasis on the first syllable) differed. Trains 1 and 2, the Dominion, the Mountaineer and the Canadian (introduced in 1955) were visually identifiable and the passengers they carried were as distinct as the train. As a youngster in that era, I poured over the details of all the trains, so I knew them well. I learned later that the names of trains were a marketing tool. The name "Dominion" suggested a train that traversed the Dominion of Canada, for instance; the "Mountaineer," the destination. CP also numbered the trains for internal use and communication ease for scheduling.

THE "STOP EVERYWHERE" WORKHORSE TRAINS

Trains 1 and 2 were daily passenger trains operating between Montreal and Vancouver, introduced to the system in 1934 with continuous service until the fall of 1955. Nicknamed "the trains that stop everywhere," these two trains were the thread that bound the country together, carrying the mail, the fast express, foodstuffs, travelling salesmen, immigrants and everyday folk who were simply travelling from point A to B. Tourists from abroad or Canadians on vacation would chose the more luxurious Dominion.

Trains 1 and 2 provided the vital connections for communities across the country, because they *did* stop everywhere. Paved highways in those days were limited and a thing of the future in rural areas. Without the train, most small communities would have been isolated. Trains 1 and 2 were the intercity trains that connected all points along the main line to the smaller villages and rural depots. The consist made for immediate identification. Trailing the locomotive was a combination of six to eight express and refrigerated cars, a couple of mail cars and a baggage car. None of the other trains had a working head end of this dimension. The mail contracts with Canada Post provided substantial income for the railway, hence the "stop everywhere" moniker.

Directly behind the baggage car were the colonist cars, basic sleeping cars that had been brought into service in the 1890s to address the huge surge in immigrants to Canada. During wartime, the colonist cars transported troops and, after the Second World War, another huge spike in immigrants from a shattered Europe. Colonist cars were basic, with wooden benches, pull-out wooden upper berths and a shared cookstove at the end of the car. Travellers brought their own food and bedding. Colonist class was rock-bottom cheap.

A day coach, tourist-class and first-class sleepers, plus a cafe car, made up the rest of the consist. Additional sleeping cars and full diners, predicated by demand, could be added or deleted as the train proceeded across the country. Trains 1 and 2 were not promoted for tourist travel as both east and westbound schedules passed through the Canadian Rockies in the dead of night. These were the "people's trains," carrying everyday folks travelling to the next town or city for appointments and shopping excursions, the travelling salesmen to work, with their huge display cases, to the next city of opportunity or families making time to visit friends and relatives in a nearby village.

Train 1 departed Windsor Station in Montreal every evening at 9:45 p.m., arriving in Sudbury at 11:35 in the morning. A connecting service from Toronto also departed Union Station every evening at 11:15 p.m. and arrived in Sudbury at 7:55 a.m. Toronto through cars were then simply added to the Montreal train and the combined train departed Sudbury at 11:55 a.m., a testimony to the well-coordinated switching operation combining the two services.

Usually leaving Montreal with a colonist car, one coach, a cafe-sleeper (with six sections and one double bedroom) and a first-class sleeper with 12 sections and one drawing room, the train travelled from Sudbury to Port Arthur and Port William (now Thunder Bay), arriving in Winnipeg the next evening.

From Winnipeg the train passed through Regina and Moose Jaw before arriving in Calgary, a 25-hour trek, stopping at all rural points along the way, delivering mail and express.

In Calgary, a massive 5900 Selkirk, Canadian Pacific's most powerful steam locomotive, was switched onto the head end. The 5900s were required to pull the train over "the big hill," railway jargon for the Rockies. In Banff, at 1:45 a.m., the locomotive would top up with a few thousand gallons of water to make steam for the arduous overnight passage through the Rockies.

Six hours later in Revelstoke, the haul through the mountain passes complete, faster but less powerful Royal Hudson locomotives replaced the mighty Selkirks for the downhill run to the coast. From Kamloops, the rail line descended into the Fraser Canyon, where some of the most incredible feats of railway construction were visible. Manpower, mules and dynamite had blasted the roadbed through Hells Gate Canyon from Spence's Bridge to Hope, BC.

Then, two hours and 40 minutes later, the four-day, cross-country journey terminated in Vancouver. From the station, ongoing passengers could transfer to overnight CP steamers that were berthed at the CPR dock adjacent to the station. Both steamers (bound for Seattle or Victoria) sailed 45 minutes after the train arrived. In 1948, trains ran on time![1]

Train 2 was the mirror image of Train 1, travelling eastward back to Montreal but with a slight anomaly in Calgary before proceeding to Regina, Winnipeg, Toronto and Montreal. Train 2 left Vancouver station at 10:00 a.m., offering long-haul travellers a morning departure. (Both Dominions and the

1 *Timetable, consist and operational information courtesy of Steve Boyko, www.traingeek.ca.*

Mountaineer in the summer departed Vancouver in early evening.) But, like its counterpart Train 1, the passage through the Rockies was in the dead of night. The train arrived in Revelstoke just after midnight, changing to a 5900 locomotive for the return journey through the Rockies.

Watching this train's arrival in Banff at 10:00 a.m. was always an event for me. On any given day, a dozen or more locals would board, off to spend a day in Calgary. It was fun to chat with the folks I knew, and I'd examine all others with curiosity, secretly wishing I could board with them.

Arrival in Calgary was at 12:45 p.m., and this was where the scheduling anomaly occurred. This daily edition of Train 2 overnighted in Calgary, leaving the following morning at 6:55 a.m. A connecting overnight service from Edmonton arrived at 6:15 a.m., having departed Edmonton at 11:55 p.m. Eastward from Calgary, the train retraced its steps back to Toronto and Montreal, adding or deleting railcars as reservations dictated between city stops. The Vancouver-to-Montreal journey was five days, the extra day a result of the overnight stop in Calgary.

For the first few years after arriving in Banff, Trains 1 and 2 were my favourites because our family often rode these trains for shopping trips, medical appointments or whatever other occasion to Calgary. The trains stopped in Canmore, Exshaw, Morley and Cochrane, and my folks invariably knew someone who boarded the train. At every stop, a whole new round of conversation began, and often half the coach occupants would gather round, like a long-lost family, catching up on everyone's news. A train trip usually meant Dad would spring for a treat like a soda pop from the newsie who walked the train selling newspapers, magazines, sandwiches, peanuts, candy bars and hot coffee from a big display tray around his neck.

Dad's system-wide family pass meant most of our travel was by train; it was free and without it we would have seldom ventured from Banff. We'd board Train 2 in Banff at 10:05 a.m., arriving in Calgary at 12:35 p.m. For most trips to Calgary, Mom packed a lunch, which we'd finish just before arrival. We seldom ate in restaurants unless it was a special occasion.

If that special occasion merited a lunch, we always ate at the Carolina Restaurant on Seventh Avenue, across from the Hudson's Bay. Only if the occasion was super special would we have dinner at the Palliser Hotel, the famous Canadian Pacific Hotel connected to the Calgary station. I can still remember the scrumptious Palliser French bread, baked fresh daily in the kitchen and served with a big pot of butter; a light and airy loaf so crusty it would shatter at the touch. To me, the rest of the meal didn't matter. After dinner, we'd lounge in big wingback chairs in the lobby until it was time to board for the return to Banff. An 11:15 p.m. departure ensured we kids would sleep all the way home, giving Mom and Dad a couple hours of peace and quiet.

Living on top of the station, I became so accustomed to the sounds of the trains that I could sleep through the night without interruption. There was one exception: Train 1. My body was so conditioned to the 1:45 a.m. arrival that, if it was on time, all was well. But if it arrived late, I'd wake every time as those few minutes' difference seemed to throw my sleep rhythms out of kilter. We also became used to the vibrations caused by the passing trains, especially the freights thundering through at track speed, shaking the whole station.

THE DOMINION

Although it had started out as a summer train, the Dominion had become Canadian Pacific's flagship passenger train in 1933, replacing the Imperial. (The outdated name had negative colonial implications for the market.) The premier service operated daily and year-round from Toronto to Vancouver, with a connecting service from Montreal. After the war, with the public flocking back to rail travel in unprecedented numbers, CP introduced two Dominion services: the Montreal Dominion and the Toronto Dominion.

A 1948 CPR timetable shows the Montreal Dominion (a.k.a. Trains 3 and 4) departing Windsor Station daily every evening at 8:00 p.m. and the Toronto Dominion (Trains 7 and 8) departing Union Station at 10:55 p.m. The Montreal Dominion arrived in Sudbury at 7:50 a.m. the following morning, 40 minutes after the arrival of the Toronto Dominion. Both trains operated from Sudbury to Vancouver only 30 to 45 minutes apart, allowing CPR's sleeping and dining car departments to juggle reservations, assigning space on either train, depending on load factor, through to Vancouver.

The Dominions differed from the 1 and 2, which were the "people's trains." Significantly, there were no head end express or mail cars. The typical consist coming into Banff then included a double-door baggage car, followed by a day coach, two tourist sleepers and a cafe car. The dining car was positioned after the cafe car, separating the first-class sleeping cars from tourist class. A first-class parlour car brought up the rear. During the summer season, an open-air observation car was added for the journey through the Rockies. The Montreal Dominion provided a small exception to the standard consist since it included a colonist car for transporting immigrants who had arrived at the port of Montreal, usually on a CP steamship. Like most major passenger railroads of the time, all railcars on the Dominions were heavyweights: all-steel construction with slab steel siding and resplendent in Canadian Pacific's signature Tuscan-red colour.

At a glance, you could easily discern the Dominions were not the "people's trains." The equipment appeared to be shinier, with better detail, and the disembarking passengers, in their formal travelling attire, also reflected the train's personality. This was the Dominion – Canadian Pacific's crack passenger train – transporting the upper class. Even the tourist-class passengers aboard – often a mix of Europeans, British and Australians on extended vacations, possibly travelling around the world with Canadian Pacific – looked more elegant. In the summer months, most would patronize the Banff Springs Hotel. The on-board staff appeared more professional too. Most of the positions were assigned by a bidding process determined by seniority, due to the tips to be made from the Dominion clientele.

Hugely exciting for me in December 1949 was the display of "new age technology" when we witnessed the first test diesel set leading the westbound Dominion, decked out in the colours of General Motors, the locomotive manufacturer. The Banff platform was packed with locals as the Dominion glided into the station – so quiet compared to the massive steam locomotives. On departure, we could feel the quiet throb of power as the train slowly began to move and, then, in a flash, it was gone! The next month we were treated to a rerun as the GM locomotive set led the eastbound Dominion back to Toronto.

The arrival of diesel power in 1951, however, marked the beginning of the end for the age of steam. By mid-1953, steam-powered passenger service on the main line was history. Although it broke many hearts to see the majestic steam locomotives fade into history, diesel power had won the day. I truly missed the massive appeal of the Selkirks, the Clydesdales of steam power, but I also experienced a growing fondness for the new diesel locomotives that were more like sleek and graceful Arabians.

Dieselization brought immediate operational changes along the main line. The same diesel set could pull the Dominion across the country to Vancouver and could fuel within the allotted times at scheduled stops. Steam locomotives had required a water stop at least every 150 miles. Maintenance and labour also favoured the diesel locomotives. While steam locomotives awaited assignment, a crew was required around the clock to keep the firebox hot and the steam pressure at operational levels. Additionally, steam locomotives had to be switched off at points across the country for maintenance or to change to a different class of locomotive.

The numerous steam locomotive changes had consumed valuable scheduling time. The diesels shaved hours off the cross-country journey, were more fuel-efficient and did not require 24-hour surveillance. By simply adding an extra remote-controlled unit, diesels could also pull much longer trains with no additional manpower. The demonstrated savings convinced CP to expedite the dieselization process ahead of schedule across the entire system.

In 1954, CP began to tweak the Dominion's operational plan and timetable in preparation for the launch of a sleek new streamliner to be introduced in 1955, leading the battle against the airlines that were siphoning off long-haul travellers. This all-new train was to become the new flagship passenger train.

Nevertheless, the Dominion would continue to play an important role in passenger service, offering first- and tourist-class accommodations, dining cars, parlour cars and day coaches. And the Dominion would still service the smaller communities on the main line bypassed in the future.

The Dominion continued to utilize the Tuscan-red heavyweight livery, but in late 1954 received a bit of a facelift. Many of the 170 or more stainless steel streamliner cars had arrived early from the manufacturer and CP used the Dominion to spark public interest by adding a mid-train Skyline dome/cafe car and a tail end Park dome car. (Tail end cars were named after Canada's national parks.) This sneak peek at the new stainless steel streamliner cars a year in advance was designed to heighten the anticipation of the launch of the new modern streamliner, and it worked.

Since its inception in 1932, the Dominion had featured the Canadian Rockies in daylight. Because the Dominion's trans-Canada journey included stops at the smaller communities, the journey from Vancouver to Montreal took 85 hours compared to 70 hours predicted for the new streamliner service. But, for the tour operators, the journey from Calgary through the Rockies continued to be a Dominion advantage and strong selling point.

THE MOUNTAINEER: A TWO-NATION TRAIN

For *me*, though, never mind the Canadian, streamlined and sparkling in stainless steel; the Mountaineer captured me from the start. Not for its looks but for its intrigue: of where it came from and who it carried.

The Mountaineer was a unique service, a two-nation train, operated by CPR and CP's US subsidiary, the Soo Line. A summer train only, it originated in St. Paul, Minnesota, and travelled west through North Dakota, crossing into Canada at North Portal, Saskatchewan. At the border it became a CP train, and the journey continued to Banff and Lake Louise and through the Canadian Rockies to Vancouver. The 2,200-mile journey was North America's longest international train route. The Mountaineer brought tens of thousands of American visitors to Canada since its introduction in 1922.

An unusual strategic alliance had formed between Canadian Pacific and American companies such as Union Pacific, the Great Northern and Northern Pacific, all bitter competitors at times during the first half of the century. The alliance bolstered ridership on *all* trains, while responding to increased demand for package tours and challenging the airline competition. The railways offered competitive interline fare agreements and created attractive circle tour itineraries, with stopovers at iconic destinations. One of the most popular tour itineraries was the Pacific Northwest and Canadian Rockies, from Chicago on Union Pacific to Sun Valley, then to Portland. Northern Pacific carried the tours to Seattle and Canadian Pacific Steamships sailed to Victoria and Vancouver. The tour groups all travelled on CP's Mountaineer through the Canadian Rockies. At Field, BC, most groups disembarked for sightseeing excursions to Takakkaw Falls and the Spiral Tunnels, crossing the Great Divide en route to Lake Louise. After a three-night stopover, the tour groups reboarded the Mountaineer in Banff for the two-night journey home to Minneapolis, Chicago and beyond. Canadian Pacific was by far the main beneficiary of this circle tour program.

Most major tour companies in the United States sold into the circle tour itineraries, but others, like Chicago-based Cartan Tours, worked outside of the alliance and featured Great Northern Railroad to Winnipeg, CNR to Jasper and motorcoach sightseeing to Lake Louise and Banff. But like all tour operators, Cartan Tours returned to Minneapolis and Chicago on the Mountaineer. Also supporting the unusual two-nation

Mountaineer were the major tour operators of the day, including Berry Tours and Cook's Tours of Boston and New York, Happiness Tours of California and Florida, Four Winds and Vanderbilt Tours of New York, Colpitts Travel of Boston, New York and Philadelphia, Laughlin Tours of Los Angeles, Frame Travel of Boston and a new entrant at that time called Tauck Tours of Connecticut, later to become the dominant tour operator in North America.

While group tours became the growth vehicle for the Mountaineer, the independent travellers, the top end of the carriage trade, "paid the freight," not unlike the first-class airline travellers of today. Wealthy families, mostly from the eastern seaboard and Florida, visited the Rockies to escape the heat, often staying three or four weeks at the Banff Springs Hotel. They travelled first class, many originating their trip in New York, Boston or Washington. Railways had invented the interline ticket; a typical ticket might read New York Central to Chicago, Chicago and North Western to Minneapolis, Soo Line to North Portal and CPR to Banff. It was no accident that, after restoring the Mountaineer service in 1947, Canadian Pacific assigned the new, sleek, flat-sided, Grove-class sleeping cars to the consist. These travellers wanted style *and* modern equipment, with mechanical air conditioning.

The first-class consist on the Mountaineer included at least two of the Tuscan-red Grove class streamliner sleeping cars, in addition to two Tuscan-red heavyweight sleepers. The Grove cars featured two different configurations: ten roomettes and five double bedrooms or a ten-compartment car. It was not unusual for one family group to book all ten compartments. The two heavyweight sleepers were also customized, offering configurations much different than the norm. One heavyweight had eight sections, one drawing room and two compartments; the other was an observation lounge and sleeper, with four double bedrooms and one compartment. A combination dining/club car and an open-air observation car completed the signature Canadian Pacific equipment. Trailing the CP equipment, the Mountaineer consist could include eight or nine deluxe Pullman sleeping cars and a couple of Pullman diners.

But the character of the train made the real difference. It was the train from America! Not only were all sleeping and dining car employees on board Americans but so were 100 per cent of the passengers. Like most of my generation, I was fascinated with Yanks (as presented by Hollywood), and in Banff we got to meet thousands of American tourists who passed through on the Mountaineer. Friendly, gregarious and generous, the US visitors arriving on the Mountaineer seemed less formal and more open than Canadians and overseas travellers, engaging in conversation without pretension.

While some adventurous Americans did drive to the Rockies on our fledging roads, others shipped their cars ahead by railway freight, picking them up after arriving in Banff, often on the Mountaineer. They could enjoy their own transportation while in Banff and then ship the cars back home. For these folks, money was not an issue. Instead of Fords or Chevrolets, the cars were luxury models, including Lincolns, Cadillacs, Buicks, DeSotos and Chryslers. I used to love to venture over to the freight shed with Dad as he released these magnificent cars to their owners – or chauffeurs. It was a world I hadn't known existed.

Buses and private cars waited at the station to greet the first-class travellers, not only from the Mountaineer but the other trains as well. Brewster provided its newest motorcoaches for the Banff Springs Hotel and private limos were often booked in advance. Most travellers had luggage checked through from their point of origin in the US, requiring customs clearance. Once again, CP accommodated the travellers, contracting with the Canadian government to have a customs officer on site throughout the summer season. Over the 14 summer seasons I lived or worked at the station, there were only two: "Fergie" Ferguson for 12 seasons and Don Donaldson for two. No doubt it was a plum posting; the position included guest-style accommodation at the Banff Springs Hotel and full dining room privileges. A career soldier until then, Fergie served as a great ambassador in Banff for Canada. He often held court in the baggage room, relating anecdotes from his days in the military. Interestingly, he never spoke of the war itself, focusing only on the good times and camaraderie he enjoyed in Canada and the United Kingdom prior to engagement.

PART II

Special Trains

HERE COME THE ROYALS

On the occasion of a royal visit, Canadian Pacific and Canadian National railways provided a mix of their best railcars, painted in a common colour scheme. A Royal Train could be ten to 12 cars long, predicated by the size of the royal entourage, security team members, accompanying dignitaries, and the UK and Canadian press. The travelling members of the royal family were assigned the best executive railcars, property of the presidents of the railways that were used for business travel and, when required, to cater to dignitaries. During a royal visit, the train travelled on both CPR and CNR rail lines and each railway assigned its own "Royal" locomotive to lead the train. Canadian Pacific, for example, renamed its Hudson class locomotives as "Royal Hudsons" after the 1939 royal visit.

The most famous royal visit to Banff might have been King George and Queen Elizabeth's in 1939. The best story about that visit involved the driver of their horse-drawn Tally-Ho, none other than Jim Brewster, the company founder and president of Brewster Transport. During the drive around the townsite, Brewster pulled into his own stately brick home located on the bank of the Bow River for afternoon tea. The only problem was he'd forgotten to inform his wife that company was coming. But Mrs. Brewster, apparently never ruffled by anything, simply pulled off the afternoon tea as if she had expected the royal couple and nothing was amiss. But I suspect Mr. Brewster heard about it later!

The royal visits of my era all occurred in the 1950s. My first experience was in October of 1951, when Princess Elizabeth and her husband Philip, then Duke of Edinburgh, toured Canada. Prior to coming to Banff, the royal couple spent a night in Calgary. It might have been the only time they could let their hair down as Mayor Don Mackay and the city provided a real western welcome, complete with a special edition of the Calgary Stampede and an evening of western entertainment, including cowboy music and square dancing. It was an evening they might have enjoyed far more than inspecting another honour guard.

The next day, Princess Elizabeth and Philip moved on to Banff for a whistle stop visit on a cold, blustery day – you could feel winter in the wind. The Royal Train arrived in Banff about 2:00 p.m. for a two-hour visit to the townsite. In 1951, especially in October, two hours was quite enough; many businesses and all attractions were closed for the season. The train came in about 20 minutes early, causing a kerfuffle as many folks missed its arrival. But my family was ready and waiting, with ringside seats on our balcony overlooking the platform only feet below. As the royal couple stepped off the train, Parks Superintendent J.A. Hutchison greet them, and then the entourage walked up the platform, entering the waiting room through the doors directly beneath our front balcony. Although the station was closed to the public, our residence must have passed the security check, so we had full views. Despite my whistling and cheering (and my mother's admonishments to silence me), the royal couple never batted an eye. We then rushed through our dining room onto our back balcony overlooking Lynx Street to see the princess and her duke boarding a big shiny Packard limousine for their tour of Banff.

Though the Banff Springs was closed for the season, the visit did include a brief stop and reception in the hotel lobby, before a drive through town to the Buffalo Paddock. Right on schedule, they were back on the train, departing for Vancouver in late afternoon. At the time, many residents questioned the decision for the Royal Train to pass through the heart of the Rockies in the dark. Apparently, those in charge of planning were more concerned about waiting dignitaries and honour-guard inspections in Vancouver than providing an enjoyable and scenic train ride for the couple through the Rockies.

Next up for the royals was Princess Margaret in July of 1958, whose visit included a short holiday in Banff partway through an official royal visit to Canada. But her Banff visit was far from the typical whistle stop tour of King George and Queen Elizabeth in 1939 and Princess Elizabeth and the Duke of Edinburgh in 1951. Both of those visits had similar itineraries: short drives around town, shaking hands with a few dignitaries and, of course, a cup of tea before reboarding the Royal Train for the next stop.

Officially, the purpose of Princess Margaret's visit to Canada was to attend British Columbia's centennial celebrations, where she was representing the Crown at various anniversary gatherings. The BC visit was followed by a coast-to-coast tour across the country, but at the end of her duties in Vancouver, Princess Margaret travelled by train to Banff to enjoy a three-day rest stop, arriving on July 26. Margaret stepped off the train to a strangely subdued crowd, according to Bill McKusker, of the *Banff Crag & Canyon*.

> Princess Margaret's arrival at Banff station Saturday night produced one of the queerest performances we can

> recall. We had expected a cheer to go up as she made her initial appearance but no, everyone just stood there and gawked. Nobody to shout, "welcome to Banff or glad to see you" or anything like that....Just a funereal silence. Adding to the general quality of fantasy which pervaded the scene was the spectacle of the white-clad princess standing on the back platform of the observation car just prior to alighting from the train and being etched against an almost black sky by hundreds of flashbulbs exploding one after another in rapid succession. Things brightened just a little bit when Margaret drove off in the car to Fairholme. Joe Brewster and yours truly were among those who were standing at the point where the road to Mt. Norquay intersects the tracks and the people around that section managed to give vent to a cheer as the princess passed. She acknowledged the greeting with a smile and wave of the hand before speeding off to Fairholme.

Sunday morning there was the requisite parade down Banff Avenue in a new Chrysler convertible. After a stop at the Cascade Gardens, the entourage drove back down the main street to a now cheering and clapping crowd. I had about a five-second glimpse as she waved from the car. I hadn't been at the station the night before for Princess Margaret's arrival, since I was by this point a teenager and our mob was having a wiener roast down at the "Rock" below the golf course. Of course, that event was much more important as we had invited several waitresses and chambermaids from the Banff Springs, along with copious amounts of beer. Wiener roasts at the Rock were always well attended by those of us who were considered minors until the age of 21 and couldn't get into the Cascade beer parlour.

The princess did do the obligatory visits, including the Cadet camp to inspect the troops and shake hands with a general or two; a stop at the Banff School of Fine Arts (now the Banff Centre) to meet the director, Donald Cameron, other Banff dignitaries, and watch ballerinas at practice; and a sightseeing visit to Mount Norquay. The highlight of the visit was Alberta Premier Ernest Manning's royal banquet at the Banff Springs Hotel on the Sunday night. My dad, the local MLA at the time, was invited to attend. It was a big moment for my folks, especially my mom, who was a dyed-in-the-wool royalist.

Dad rented a spiffy tuxedo especially for the occasion and Mom bought a new dinner dress. All my sisters came home for the event, helping Mom get ready and tying Dad's bow tie. I remember how we all gathered around the living room that night as they regaled us with stories of being presented to the princess, the magnificent six-course dinner and the rest of the pomp and ceremony.

In a departure from most royal visits, Princess Margaret stayed in the privacy of the Fairholme Ranch. (Due to a threat of bomb blasts in BC from the Sons of Freedom Doukhobor sect, the princess was accompanied by a security detail made up of 132 Mounties – if that can be considered privacy). The Fairholme Ranch was located east of Banff, tucked in the forest off the Johnson Lake road, overlooking the Bow Valley toward Mount Rundle. The ranch house was owned by Captain O'Brien-ffrench, the Marquis de Castelthomond. His life story read like an action novel. In his early adult years, he had been a Mountie with the Royal North West Mounted Police, and during the Second World War he was known as Agent 23 with the British secret service. After the war, captured German secret service files indicated O'Brien-ffrench had been on the Gestapo hit list. Another agent with the British secret service, novelist Ian Fleming, apparently based his James Bond character on O'Brien-ffrench. In 1946, O'Brien-ffrench purchased one of the few remaining parcels of freehold land in the national park from the Anthracite Coal Company, where he designed and built his classic log home. During Princess Margaret's visit, he moved out of Fairholme, offering his residence for the duration of her stay.

Princess Margaret's visit was followed a year later by another whistle stop tour by Queen Elizabeth and Prince Philip on July 10, 1959. That time, the Royal Train arrived in Banff shortly before 10:00 a.m. On instructions from Her Majesty, the train was stopped about 100 yards short of the official disembarking point so she could review the assembled Boy Scouts, Girl Guides, Cubs and Brownies. Instead of me, they were the ones to get the best view of the royal couple. Harry Dempster, superintendent of Banff National Park, welcomed and accompanied the royal couple for a short drive through town in a Brewster touring car, driven by Walter Ashdown, Brewster's senior chauffeur.

I was working at the station as a redcap, but the authorities kept us off the platform when the Royal Train arrived, so I rode my bike downtown to view the parade from the sidewalk along Banff Avenue. I arrived just minutes before the royal entourage and was quite surprised at the sparse crowd; I had imagined throngs of people cheering their monarch. There was no problem to get a front and centre view on the sidewalk in front of the Texaco service station as the big shiny Chrysler convertible drove by. A few hundred people did line the main street but were subdued and polite, only offering a smattering of applause. The tour route took Queen Elizabeth and Prince Philip up Banff Avenue to the Administration Grounds, and then back down, to the delight of the assembled spectators. The next stops were short visits to the Banff School of Fine Arts and the Cadet camp to meet the military brass and inspect more cadets. Then the queen and prince were whisked away to Lake Louise, where about a thousand royal admirers were on hand. After a tour of the chateau, General Manager D.A. Williams hosted lunch before the royals departed for the Field station, where they reboarded the Royal Train and departed for Vancouver.

I always wondered why the royal route around Banff always took in the same old boring stuff when there was so much more to enjoy around "Banff the Beautiful," even during a whistle stop visit. Lake Minnewanka, Vermilion Lakes and Mount Norquay all offered spectacular sights and were well within a two-hour time frame, and a stroll down picturesque Banff Avenue would have been an excellent venue to meet the adoring crowds. I guess the local big shots and the generals playing army with kids were far more important than meeting with the people and showing off a wonder of the world. Bill McKusker of the *Crag & Canyon* agreed with me in his editorial headlined "Nauseating Farce."

> Royal Tours of the type currently taking place are a farce – a nauseating farce and there should be no more of them. The spectacle of two human beings being paraded before the populace by minor functionaries is enough to bring feelings of disgust to even the most avid of curiosity seekers....We wonder whether it would not be feasible to let them come to Banff, say, and spend

as much time as they liked in this mountain paradise, doing as they pleased, WHEN they pleased...and with a minimum of attendants.

The Royal Trains were very special and hugely entertaining for the public, but they only occurred once or twice in a generation. However, over the years, Canadian Pacific created its own market for "special trains" that fed competitions, events and festivals across the country. These special trains were complete trains, some with day coaches only, transporting passengers to nearby day events. But the most exciting were the long-distance specials, with sleeping, dining and parlour cars, transporting passengers across the country to an event of national interest such as the Grey Cup.

THE GREY CUP SPECIAL

Every year, in late November, Canadian Pacific operated special football trains for the fans from the cities whose teams would compete in the Grey Cup. These trains and the antics of the travelling fans often made headlines when they arrived at the host city.

The Grey Cup trains began in November of 1948 when the Calgary Stampeders won the Western Division and travelled to Toronto to meet the home team Argonauts. A special train was organized for Calgary fans and quickly sold out. Over 280 fans were on board for the three-day journey. A few surprises were in store for the folks in Toronto as many Calgarians brought their horses with them for the Grey Cup Parade. Freight cars were specially outfitted to transport the horses, bringing the Wild West to downtown Toronto. Two horses were ridden up the front steps and into the lobby of the Royal York Hotel, causing controversy in a city known as "Toronto the Good." Calgary was to go on and win its first Grey Cup that year.

After that precedent-setting year, the Grey Cup Special became an integral part of the Grey Cup celebrations. In 1958, the Winnipeg Blue Bombers won the western championship to meet the eastern champion Hamilton Tiger-Cats at Empire Stadium in Vancouver, only the second time in the history of Canadian football that the Grey Cup had been played in the west. Sometime after school started in September, I learned that my friends Gordon and Russell Standish were going to stay with their aunt in Vancouver because their dad had access to tickets for the game. Then Jim Alexander announced that he too was going and convinced me I should join the fun. Apprehensive about asking for permission, I was gobsmacked when Dad immediately agreed it was a great opportunity. Dad even went to the station to see if he could help with our train reservations. We figured we'd end up on the Dominion in a tourist sleeping car with a couple of upper and lower berths but found ourselves in a compartment in a first-class car on the Winnipeg Grey Cup Special! Sixteen years old and we'd be in the middle of the action.

The train arrived mid-afternoon on Thursday, November 27, and boarding was immediate as we were the only Banff passengers ticketed. The train was 12 cars long, with a day coach, nine sleepers, a dining car and club car. The sleeping car porter who showed us to our compartment said, "You boys won't be getting much sleep tonight. This whole train is crazy!" It was soon apparent that our car was party central; some of the portable compartment walls had been removed and rabid Winnipeg supporters were well into their second day of partying. What a night it was for the boys from Banff.

We arrived in Vancouver early Friday morning at Waterfront Station, overlooking the piers for the huge CP steamships and the Victoria and Seattle ferries. The previous summer Jim and I had checked hundreds of pieces of luggage for passengers travelling onward from Vancouver to Victoria or Seattle, or even a CP ship destined for Alaska, never imagining we'd ever be in Vancouver. I almost had to pinch myself to make sure I wasn't dreaming.

Gordon and Russell's aunt met us on arrival and sensed we were completely smitten by the city, so we set off on a walking tour of the downtown before taking a short bus ride to her home. That evening, we returned to the downtown core to view the pre-game events and Grey Cup madness. Most of the activity surrounded the intersection of Granville and Georgia streets near the famous beer parlour of the Georgia Hotel. Our mission that evening was to talk our way into the pub. I was more than nervous, imagining doom and cop scenarios if we were caught out as the minors we were. It was needless apprehension; the queue to get in the pub was around the block.

The Grey Cup game was played Saturday afternoon, November 29, and 35,000 people were jammed into Empire Stadium, at that time the largest crowd in Grey Cup history. We were all cheering for Winnipeg, but in the first quarter Hamilton went ahead 14 – 0. Winnipeg stormed back, leading 21 – 14 at halftime and won the game 35 – 28. Like us, the pro-western crowd was delirious, and thousands stayed on in the stadium, cheering and clapping long after the game was over. My first trip away from home without my parents, travelling on a crazy Grey Cup Special, my first visit to Vancouver and my first live football game – all in one package!

After the game, we boarded a bus back to the city centre, but the driver had to stop a couple of blocks from Waterfront Station. The party had spread downtown and the crowds had plugged Granville Street, blocking all approaches to the station. We walked the last few blocks through the throng and what I remember was the mood of the crowd – boisterous but not violent or obnoxious. It was all good fun.

Our train departed in early evening, but the passengers on this train were subdued. We had been ticketed back to Banff, again in our own compartment, but this time on the Hamilton Grey Cup Special. We kept our heads down and mouths shut. There were no parties, just a few miserable drunks.

The adventure of our last night on the train was dinner in

the diner. Jim and I were flush with money from our summer jobs in the baggage room, so it was to be our treat. Envisioning some sort of fancy dining experience, we were in trouble right off the bat. It was a table d'hôte menu and none of us had any idea what that meant. The waiter, doing his best to maintain his composure, explained it was a fixed price menu, that we could have soup or salad, appetizer, main course and dessert. Happily, we ordered everything, but then the surprises began. The waiter, with great aplomb, placed empty soup bowls in front of us and then disappeared. Now we were definitely confused, wondering what was the scoop on the soup? Where were the crackers? Did we go and get our own? The couple across the aisle were greatly amused, saying, "He'll be back shortly with the tureen." Tureen? What was that? I turned to Jim, "Did we order tureen?" thinking it might be some kind of fish. He shrugged, "I don't know, but we've got all kinds of knives and forks, so it must be lots of food."

By the time the waiter arrived back with the tureen, ladling out the soup, the couple across the aisle were in near hysterics from listening to our conversation. Following the soup was some sort of appetizer, which I don't recall, but I well remember the main course. I think the dining car staff, understanding we were completely intimidated, decided to make it up to us via our stomachs. We were presented with huge slabs of prime rib that covered our plates. With a nod and a wink, our waiter motioned toward the galley and there stood the chef, sporting a big smile and giving us a wave. He must have been a Winnipeg fan!

We arrived back in Banff late Sunday afternoon flush from our Grey Cup experience. The Vancouver stories were the buzz at school for the next couple of days and got better and better as we retold in detail the magic of our Grey Cup experience. But we did not mention the tureen.

THE BANFF SPRINGS HOTEL STAFF TRAINS

Perhaps the most bizarre of special trains were the annual Banff Springs Hotel staff trains that transported the employees back home to Ontario and eastern Canada at the end of the season. Both the Banff Springs and the Chateau Lake Louise were seasonal operations and hired the bulk of their staff from the east. Free round-trip transportation was part of the employment agreement and a huge incentive to keep your job. If an employee was fired or resigned prior to the end of the season, the return ticket was cancelled. CP Hotels definitely understood the benefit of long-distance hiring, holding the threat of cancellation over the employee's head. Until the Banff Springs opened on a year-round basis, few employees hailed from the west. I myself had never entertained the thought of working at the hotel.

When the staff trains arrived in the spring, I remember them as relatively subdued. Most staff were college students. They arrived broke, were keen to get to work and had yet to make their summer friendships. But the staff specials at the end of the season were a different creature: a combination of chaos, tears and broken hearts, with some heavy-duty partying thrown into the mix.

The return specials ran on two consecutive days, operating as a second section of the eastbound Dominion. Both trains were packed, transporting the thousand-plus staff members home. The train consist usually included a day coach, a cafe car, up to a dozen tourist sleepers and two baggage cars required to haul the inordinate amount of luggage. Most staff had two or three pieces of luggage, which created a separate nightmare for us baggage room attendants. In early afternoon, the deluge began. Baggage buses began arriving at the station full of boxes, suitcases, steamer trunks and kit bags. By 5 p.m. a mountain of luggage filled the baggage room. As departing staff arrived to check their luggage, it quickly turned into a zoo. Many were already inebriated, had no idea where they were or couldn't find their train tickets, which were required to check the luggage, let alone which luggage was theirs to identify. As a result, on every departure, we always had to grapple with untagged luggage, simply piling it in the baggage car. Fortunately, there was lots of time between Banff and Toronto to sort out the mess.

When the train arrived at the platform, the reality of departure set in and the tears of young love would begin to flow: hugging, wailing and kissing, all professing everlasting love to the one who was left behind or travelling on the next day's train. True trauma could also occur annually for some unfortunate young ladies who would now have to face Mom and Dad on their own to explain their pregnancies.

Over the years I had met several sleeping car porters who worked the Dominion and the Canadian. Every fall, one of the older porters would bid to work a staff train, always successful, as few of his colleagues wanted any part of the chaos. When I asked him why, he explained that after the first night of the partying, antics and tears, the remainder of the journey was quite enjoyable. He'd have the opportunity to sit and talk with the young folk and found them much more interesting and far less demanding than the regular traffic with whom the company actually discouraged engagement. He also reported the financial reward; at the end of the trip the kids tipped over the top as they themselves had relied on tips all summer. But he mostly enjoyed being with the young people who were embarking on their next journey in life.

I had watched this scene for years, first as a kid from our balcony and then during the seven years I worked at the station. The script never changed. But the insight passed along to me by the sleeping car porter gave me pause to look at things from a slightly different perspective.[2]

2 The staff trains were cancelled when the famous hotel opened on a year-round basis in 1968. The hiring practices changed completely as year-round professional staff were then engaged and the hotel was no longer dependent on students for its summer operation. It was literally the end of an era.

THE BANFF WINTER CARNIVAL SPECIAL

In the early years, Banff wasn't considered a major winter resort. Ski Trains from Calgary had disappeared in the early 50's and Mt. Norquay stayed predominantly a local ski club even after George Encil had built its first chairlift (and first in Canada) in 1949. (Skiing would remain a pursuit for locals and hardy weekenders from Calgary until the 1960s and the major developments at Sunshine Village and Lake Louise ski areas.)

Nevertheless, Christmas in Banff was a holiday dream for many. Although the Banff Springs was closed, the Mount Royal, Cascade and King Edward hotels filled with Christmas and New Year's visitors. Additionally, there were some impressive vacation homes in Banff in the days prior to the "need to reside" legislation. The Graham family of Vancouver owned a huge mansion-style home on Cave Avenue. Its patriarch, F.R. Graham, was one of the major financiers and industrialists in the province and owned Union Steamships, the forerunner to BC Ferries. In 1848, he had founded Graymont Ltd., an international company supplying limestone products around the world. The family's entourage, including 12 children and many friends, arrived by train and was met by Brewster private cars assigned to the family through to the New Year. It was considered a social coup for a Banffite to snag an invitation to the Graham's annual New Year's Eve bash. Riding on my parent's coattails, I did manage to attend the New Year's Eve party in 1961. I had never seen such a display of food in my life and the champagne flowed freely.

But the most exciting event of the winter was the annual Winter Carnival. It was certainly popular as a week of fun and celebration for us locals, but the event was created in 1917 to attract winter visitation and inject some much-needed capital into the community during the dead of winter. For many decades, in January, the excitement began to build as the February dates approached. For example, on December 30, 1917, the *Crag & Canyon* reported,

> Between twenty and thirty representative business men met at the Fire Hall Thursday night to informally discuss the feasibility of holding a winter carnival in Banff. The meeting was very enthusiastic, and sites and finance committees were named to report at a public meeting on Tuesday night. The government has promised support in the way of *alien labor* [prisoners of war] for the ice palace, etc. The plan is to stage the carnival in February, during the bonspiel week, through the following weekend. If pulled off, it should greatly benefit Banff.

Did they ever pull it off! From the beginning, the carnival organizers thought big, organizing a two-week event, targeting visitors from Manitoba, Saskatchewan, Alberta and British Columbia. The first carnival kicked off on February 6, 1917, opening with the Banff Bonspiel, followed by another week of competitive winter sports, including skiing, tobogganing, ice boating, speed and figure skating and swimming contests at the Cave and Basin. First and second prizes were awarded in all events, as well as trophies and cups. An ice palace was constructed on the riverbed below the Bow River Bridge, and a maze for kids was built from ice blocks cut from the Bow

River and located in the intersection in front of the present-day Canadian Imperial Bank of Commerce.

From the beginning, Canadian Pacific had been a supporter and sponsor, offering special discounted rates to Banff from towns and cities across Canada. Canadian Pacific extended the special rates throughout the carnival years and helped subsidize the travel expenses of the carnival queen candidates who came from Winnipeg, Regina, Calgary, Edmonton, Revelstoke and Vancouver. As the reputation of the carnival grew, prospective queens and visitors were attracted from as far away as Seattle, Portland, California and even Quebec City. In the late 1940s and early 1950s, the Banff Winter Carnival continued to grow in stature, eventually being declared as one of two major winter events in Canada (the other being the Quebec Winter Carnival).

Each year "the government" was a major participant, building the ice palace and skating rink on the Bow River and the toboggan slide from St. Julien Road, down Caribou Street, to its terminus at the Mount Royal Hotel. Beginning in early January, the snow on Caribou Street was ploughed into the middle of the street and, then, in early February, wooden forms were inserted to shape the slide. Once shaped, the slide was iced down nightly. The toboggan slide was a highlight of the carnival, especially for the Banff kids. A ride cost only five cents, but you had to pull your toboggan up to the top on St. Julien Road. Or you might get lucky and have Eddie Evans tow you behind his 1948 Anglia.

On a cold, crisp day or night, when the chute was nicely iced, your toboggan would blast through the Beaver Street intersection and into bales of hay scattered on the roadway to stop the toboggans from hurtling onto Banff Avenue. On competition day, the toboggan races were timed events. The teams pulled their toboggans to the top of the slide, into the chute and flew down to the bottom. Contest categories included teams from junior high, senior high and the general public.

One of the most popular spectator events was the annual carnival regatta held at the Cave and Basin swimming pool, which the government would open especially for the carnival. Aquatic events, including synchronized swimming, swimming races and canoeing contests, were held and the attendance was in the hundreds as evidenced in photos.

Over the years, the reputation and popularity of the Banff Winter Carnival spread far and wide, attracting more and more long-stay visitors. Each year Canadian Pacific continued to offer special fares to Banff and the downtown hotels offered similar carnival packages. For over 40 years, visitors breathed new life into Banff's economy when it was most needed. In 1952, the carnival added a new dimension to the week-long event. Under the leadership of Banff businessman Early Gammon, the 1890s boom town theme of Silver City was constructed on the ice of the Bow River in front of the current location of the Whyte Museum. Food stalls sold hot dogs and elk burgers, and storefronts housing tent saloons provided hot coffee and wheels of chance. Spin the wheel, win a prize. Red Crozier, a colourful local character, was appointed sherriff for the duration of the carnival, and he raised hundreds of dollars "arresting" businessmen and citizens and then selling their freedom at mock trials. The freewheeling fun was hugely popular and successful. For evening entertainment, the Silver City theme continued with entertainment in the Rocky Mountain Tours garage, the current location of the Grizzly House restaurant.

In the early 1950s, the carnival had attracted the attention of the Calgary newspapers, which promoted its entertainment value to Calgarians. Don Mackay, Calgary's famous "white hat" mayor and weekend Banff resident, also jumped on the bandwagon, offering moral and financial support. Canadian Pacific began operating the Banff Winter Carnival Special from Calgary, transporting bands, carnival queen candidates and hundreds of fun seekers to Banff on the Saturday, which was eventually called Calgary Day. Calgary's Junior Chamber of Commerce (JCs) teamed up with the Banff JCs to become the train's sponsor.

In 1955, Dalyce Smith, from Whitehorse, Yukon, was chosen as carnival queen to reign over the 1956 Banff Winter Carnival. Later that spring, Dalyce was also chosen as Miss Canada, giving the carnival an extra media boost, as she announced she would return to Banff to reign over the 1956 carnival. "Banff Winter Carnival Queen Crowned Miss Canada" headlined many newspapers across the country.

By the mid-1950s, the Carnival Special was well entrenched, carrying over 500 people per trip. As the popularity of the train grew, the carnival attracted more Calgary sponsors. But, in October 1958, the Banff Chamber of Commerce, which had operated the carnival in 1957 and 1958, held a secret ballot vote regarding its continued participation in the event. In an almost unanimous decision, the chamber members voted not to operate the carnival in 1959. According to the *Crag & Canyon* of November 19, 1958,

> [The] proposal that an entirely new body be set up to run the Banff Winter Carnival and other major sports events in Banff was unanimously endorsed at the annual meeting of the Banff Chamber of Commerce. A meeting of the heads of various organizations in Banff will

> be called to establish and incorporate the new body. The proposal was given earnest support by Mayor Don Mackay of Calgary, one of the speakers at the meeting.

It seemed to be a great idea at the time, but the first meeting called by the chamber to establish the new body attracted only a few attendees. A second attempt to form the organization was called for early December and was advertised as the final attempt to gain traction. The threat seemed to work, and an executive was formed. The results of the meeting were published in the December 3 edition of the *Crag & Canyon*.

> J. Paul Richer, office manager for C.B. Brewster Enterprises, was named chairman of the 1959 Banff Winter Carnival last night at a meeting attended by over 40 representatives of local organizations and interested individuals. Elected to the executive were Fred Wonnacott, Ron Scott and Corky Pederson. The names of Bert Hynes and Charlie Masur were also put forward but since neither was present at the meeting their choices could not be confirmed.

This may have been an omen; both Bert Hynes and Charlie Masur had been huge contributors to the success of past winter carnivals.

Dates for the carnival were set back a couple of weeks later than usual, with Thursday, February 26, chosen as the opening date. The committees felt they would require extra time to organize due to the delay in creating the new organization. For the first time ever, a Calgary committee for the carnival had been established, led by Mayor Mackay. From the *Crag & Canyon* on January 21, 1959:

> Mr. Jim McLeod, parade chairman, outlined plans for the Saturday parade and the arrival of the Calgary special train. Mr. George Ho Lem, representing the Calgary Junior Chamber of Commerce, stated that they would once again sponsor the train, with a target of 600 people. Plans were made to carry a special jive band to play at the Teen Town jive session Saturday afternoon and evening. This would allow the young people in town to take part in the carnival and lessen the danger of rowdiness that might occur as a result of inactivity.

Prophetic words indeed!

The Carnival Special was a smashing success, carrying over 600 Calgarians, the reigning carnival queen and the queen contestants to Banff. In Canmore, the train made a stop, picking up the carnival princesses from Banff, who were led aboard by the Princess Patricia's Canadian Light Infantry Band. The carnival princesses welcomed the passengers and, upon arrival at the Banff station, the band, the queen, her court and all the passengers marched in a parade into downtown Banff. Unfortunately, they marched into a soggy, wet, downtown Banff.

There had been a slight problem with Mother Nature. On Friday afternoon, an exceptionally warm chinook wind blasted into the Bow Valley. By Saturday morning, the meltdown had taken its toll, and the intensity of the chinook continued through the day. The ice sculptures were the first to go, melting to unrecognizable blobs. Mount Norquay, Mather's Skating Rink and the natural ice at the old curling rink were affected next, causing the cancellation of the ski races, figure and speed skating competitions and prematurely ending the mixed bonspiel. With literally nothing left to do for the largest crowd that had ever attended a winter carnival, many chose to drink. By late afternoon, the 100 and 200 blocks of Banff Avenue had turned into an ugly drunken mob scene, resulting in over 50 arrests. The Cascade, Mount Royal and King Edward all suffered major room damage as vandals ripped sinks off the walls, flooding many of the rooms, ruining carpets and furniture. For a few hours it was bedlam. Immediately after the carnival closed on the Sunday, the hue and cry began to terminate the winter carnival.

The victim of a late start date, possibly some poor planning and a wild chinook, the Banff Winter Carnival was never to be again. Personally, I was devastated. Every year I had eagerly awaited the carnival and couldn't believe that this was the end, expecting there would be some sort of last-minute reprieve and the carnival would be resurrected. The unity of the Banff residents appeared to have fractured over the 1959 carnival fiasco, but, in reality, it had been a long time coming. Changes were afoot as ski area development began to expand the winter season, and many of the new breed of businessmen felt the winter carnival was too much work for too small of a gain and no longer the vehicle to attract winter business. But the biggest loss was of the carnival spirit that had bound the community together for so many years. The business community was divided and Parks Canada, whose support had already started to waver, now had an easy out. But, while it lasted, the residents of Banff had proudly produced a major Canadian event.

In a final touch of irony, the most successful Banff Winter Carnival Special Train in the event's 41-year history was also the last, shunted aside to the history books.

THE PARTNERS: FROM STATION TO VILLAGE TO RESORT

After the completion of the railway in November 1885, Cornelius Van Horne had turned his focus to the construction of Canadian Pacific's resort hotels across the country, especially the Banff Springs Hotel, which opened its doors in 1888. A savvy marketer, Van Horne and his campaign to sell the spectacular Canadian Rockies took the US and European markets by storm. He had created a Canadian Pacific brand that was so powerful it became synonymous with Canada. But the company was nevertheless aware that strong partnerships had to be developed at the destination to provide the infrastructure servicing the attractions required to promote and sell a successful resort.

Consistent, reliable carriage service was a must from the train station to the Banff Springs Hotel, along with dependable outfitters and guides catering to the guests. Since all sightseeing and exploring had to be by horseback at that time, the manager at the Banff Springs at first scrabbled together a loosely organized group of guides but soon realized that a dedicated, contracted operator was the necessary solution. He then approached his friend John Brewster, owner of the local dairy farm. John offered the services of his two eldest sons, Jim and Bill, barely in their teens. Initially offering guiding services and fishing trips, the brothers later established a horse-drawn Tally-Ho coach service to meet all trains and provide transfers to the hotel. In 1914, when the national park was opened to vehicular travel,

Brewster was first in line with motorized touring cars and introduced the first buses in the 1920s.

The Brewster – Canadian Pacific partnership grew exponentially over the years, resulting in concession privileges for Brewster at Canadian Pacific properties, including the train stations in Calgary, Banff, Lake Louise and Field. The railway on numerous occasions even provided financing for Brewster's expansion, and rescued the company from financial disaster following the First World War. Brewster's fortunes did turn for the better until confronted with competition from ex-employee J.I. McLeod and his Rocky Mountain Tours and Transport and a struggle for sightseeing supremacy in the mountain national parks.

Brewster always had a leg up on the competition, however, because of its exclusive livery rights with Canadian Pacific to pick up and drop off at the Banff, Calgary, Lake Louise and Field train stations. Rocky Mountain Tours could drop its passengers at the station, but when picking up had to park its buses on the edge of the property line and walk its clients across the parking lot. Luggage also had to be transported to the street, which was more inconvenient for the customer.

While living at the station, I witnessed a particularly ugly day, with gusting winds and pouring rain, when a tour escort balked at walking his group off the platform and into the downpour. He demanded the Rocky Mountain Tours driver pull up to the platform and load. That's when the day got uglier. The Brewster agent on duty, assisted by a couple of his drivers, attempted to block the group from boarding the bus. Rocky Mountain's tour escort, a burly college student resembling a linebacker, literally swung into action and started a melee. Finally, the CPR constable arrived on the scene and separated the combatants, allowing the group to load from the platform and quickly depart. Livery rights were zealously guarded. Even though Rocky Mountain Tours had newer equipment, Brewster's rights with the CPR often won the day in any competition for new business.

Both Brewster and Rocky Mountain Tours and Transport had been well positioned to meet the challenge when Banff experienced the unprecedented boom in tourism after the war and the Banff Springs and the Chateau Lake Louise re-opened. The Mountaineer train service from Chicago, St. Paul and Minneapolis was reinstated in 1947 and, by 1949, the number of passengers exceeded even the golden years of the 1920s. The Banff-Jasper highway opened, with the Columbia Icefield becoming the latest Rockies attraction. However, as costs including wages, fuel and new equipment increased, the total business was not enough to maintain two identical services in a 90-day season. In 1957, Brewster Transport and Rocky Mountain Tours and Transport amalgamated, ending a 36-year battle for survival.

Over those years, however, the marketing efforts of the two competitors had assisted CP in boosting the visibility of the Canadian Rockies by focusing on the American tour companies. Officially, the ironclad livery contracts made Brewster the most favoured son, but unofficially both companies were viewed positively as strong partners by the railway. And why not? Canadian Pacific had the most to gain. Everyone had to ride its trains.

Reliable transportation, sightseeing services and quality outfitters were not the only partners required to support the year-round train service to Banff. Since the Banff Springs Hotel was closed from early September to late May, other accommodations were necessary for off-season travellers, as well as visitors who could not afford the tariff at the Banff Springs Hotel. Thus, the downtown properties and businesses, catering to the middle class and year-round visitors, became CP's most important partners and were viewed as complementary. In fact, CP consciously encouraged development of the townsite.

The Banff Springs was not a CP "partner" – it *was* the CPR and its story will not be told here. Many fine books have been published, but Bart Robinson's *Banff Springs: The Story of a Hotel* is one of the best reads on this subject. This history is entertaining, and the anecdotes are priceless. When I was living far from Banff, Bart's book was my go-to remedy to cure the occasional twinge of homesickness. I couldn't even guess how many times I've thumbed through that book.

In 1888, the Wells family opened the Alberta Hotel, Banff's first "downtown" hotel. In 1904, directly across the street, Banff pioneer Norman Luxton opened the King Edward Hotel. Luxton also owned the King Edward Livery and Stables, an early competitor for Brewster Transport. The original hotel burned to the ground but was replaced with a red brick structure in 1920, a famous Banff landmark that also housed the Lux Theatre.

Dave and Annie McDougall of the famous Reverend McDougall family of Morley built the Mount Royal Hotel in 1908. Jim Brewster purchased it in 1912. The hotel was an immediate success and a lucrative investment for his young and growing company. Shortly after the purchase, Brewster enlarged the dining room and added 50 guest rooms. The Mount Royal became the premier downtown property that featured a main floor veranda that extended the length of the Banff Avenue and Caribou Street frontages and a sweeping second-story balcony that overlooked the downtown landscape.

After the repeal of prohibition in 1924 in Alberta, breweries entered the hotel business, since liquor laws required all licensed premises to have at least ten hotel rooms for overnight guests. That began a spree of hotel purchases and construction as the competing breweries scrambled to corner the beer market via ownership of the dispensaries called "beer parlours." Often the rooms were less than basic, built to conform to the letter of the law. In Banff, Calgary Breweries bought the King Edward and the original Cascade hotels, thereby giving it about 80 per cent of the draught beer market in town. A small beer parlour in the Mount Royal was its only competition. For years, Alberta's breweries were content to be in the beer business, viewing their rooms as a small but necessary annoyance. In Banff, that meant the Mount Royal continued to be the downtown property of choice.

By 1948, Calgary Breweries had changed its attitude and rebuilt the Cascade Hotel, catering to overnight visitors as well as the tavern clientele. The "new" Cascade was advertised as the most modern hotel in Banff, boasting a coffee shop, dining room, a solarium for private functions and the famous Cascade beer parlour, with men only and ladies and escorts taverns, separated by a dividing wall. Access for men to the ladies' side meant they had to be escorting a lady. Next door was the Cascade Dance Hall, a separate business entity but a good neighbour for the evening crowds.

Summer and winter, the downtown properties met all train arrivals with their own shuttle buses. While the passenger numbers to Banff were slim compared to summer volumes, holiday periods, long weekends, the North American Ski Championships and the Banff Winter Carnival kept the town buzzing. From Vancouver, the train was super convenient, offering a choice of two early evening departures: at 7:35 or 8:15 p.m. After a pleasant evening socializing in the club car and a good sleep in your roomette or compartment, you awoke in time for breakfast in the Rockies and an afternoon arrival in Banff, where a transfer coach and a hotel representative greeted you. It was a convenient downtown-to-downtown service. Plus, rail travel, including the sleeping accommodation, was not expensive.

While not open year-round, the Homestead Hotel was another hotel that opened earlier and closed later than the Banff Springs. Only two short blocks from the station and one block from the centre of town, the Homestead enjoyed a favoured reputation with returning visitors. The hotel was a classic wooden structure, with balconies and verandas. Set beside the main building was the Homestead Hotel Annex and the famous Homestead Restaurant and Tea Room (the site currently occupied by Melissa's Restaurant).

When we moved to Banff, the Homestead instantly became our favourite restaurant to recommend when visitors came to town, largely because owners Earl and Enid Gammon were long-time friends of Mom and Dad. Although Earl had worked for Brewster before and after enlisting in the Canadian Army, he left to start Gammon Construction Company in Cochrane, where he'd met Mom and Dad.[3] The Gammons were our

3 *Gammon was hugely successful in the construction business, with many firsts in Alberta. He built the Glenmore Dam and the York Hotel in Calgary and, while owner of the Black Diamond Coal Company, built the first paved highway in the province, from Calgary to Coal Creek. He also paved the runway of the old Calgary Municipal Airport, the first paved airstrip in the country.*

welcome wagon when we moved to Banff in 1948. A daily fixture during the years we lived at the station, Earl would always park his car of the day at the platform in front of the express office. He loved big fast cars, especially his 1936 V-12 Packard Phaeton, said to have been a "mob car" in Chicago. The station newsstand was his morning coffee stop where he and Dad joined their cronies for the latest from around town. He'd allow admirers like me to inspect his pride and joy, and regale us with stories of Al Capone and the car's fascinating history.

In 1955, addressing the need for more hotel space and anticipating the automobile boom accompanying the construction of the Trans-Canada, Earl built the Gammon Motel, directly across the street from the Homestead (on the site now occupied by the Banff Park Lodge). Billed as a deluxe motor inn, it was an immediate success. Gammon was an excellent marketer, a visionary and active politically. A huge supporter of the Banff Winter Carnival, Earl was president in 1952 and 1953 for two of the most successful carnivals ever staged. He had a larger than life profile as an active Rotarian and president of the regional association of the Conservative Party. He was a valuable partner and tireless promoter for Banff and the Canadian Rockies.

COMMUNICATIONS CENTRAL

Through the mid '50s – even in a growing resort town like Banff – many homes and most staff residences still did not have telephones. Letters, postcards and aerograms (a lightweight sheet of paper that folded into its own envelope) were the norm. Even businesses avoided doing business by telephone; it was expensive and cumbersome. A long-distance call required the local operator to contact a long-distance operator who would then route the call through a series of other operators across the country until the call reached its destination. But CP Telecommunications was there with the solution of the day.

Business communication was largely conducted by telegraph, electronically transmitted in Morse code. Canadian Pacific had its own telegraph and telephone lines across Canada and, depending on the importance of the message, you could send a day letter with guaranteed same-day delivery, or a night letter, sent after 6:00 p.m., that would be delivered the following morning. Most businesses usually communicated by the more expensive day letters, allowing for same-day response. Night letters were most often personal communications sent by the public and were cheaper. Delivery on the other end was either by telephone, with a hard copy to follow, or hand-delivered to the addressee if they did not have a telephone.

Banff had two telegraph offices in the winter and three in the summer. The downtown location was in the Brewster Head Office building, just off Banff Avenue on Caribou Street, open daily from 8:00 a.m. to 5:00 p.m. In the summer, another office was open in the lobby of the Banff Springs. The main office was in the station. This office included the telephone office, the call centre for all CP operations in Banff, including the Banff Springs and the Chateau Lake Louise. Although the hotels had their own in-house telephone exchange, all incoming and outgoing long-distance calls were routed through the station operators.

During the years we lived at the station, Betty Mewburn and Betty Davidson were the senior telephone agents. Their world was a fascinating place to visit as they made the connections with other operators in cities across Canada and the United States. Direct dialing was still in the future. My sister Frances worked a summer in the telephone office and still remembers calls from celebrities, including movie stars Alan Young and Alan Ladd – very exciting stuff for a Banff teenager!

On winter evenings, I'd often wander downstairs to visit with the on-duty operator and telegrapher. Bill Timinsky had the second "trick" (4:00 p.m. to midnight shift) and had figured out how to keep me occupied, teaching me Morse code. My dad had got his start with the railway this way, and my dream then was to be an operator like him. Bill set me up with a practice telegraph key in the corner of the office. Memorizing the code was easy; the alphabet consists of dots and dashes or a combination of both. But transmitting or receiving a live message was much more difficult, requiring hours of practice on the "key" and listening to the telegraph sounder that relayed the messages. When I was 11 years old, I got my first crack at transmitting; Bill had me send the nightly weather report, which consisted of a series of numbers in code describing current temperatures, wind velocity, precipitation and barometer settings. Heady stuff for an aspiring young operator.

Mr. Culley, our local weatherman, brought the weather report to the station every evening. He had all sorts of gadgets set up near the Buffalo Paddock east of town: anemometers, barometers, thermometers and various containers to measure precipitation. But little did he know his weather report was sometimes sent by an 11-year-old kid. I've often wondered if I ever made a mistake telegraphing his numbers that might have revealed Banff as the hot spot in North America in January!

When proficient with the telegraph key, you'd graduate to the "bug." The bug was introduced not only to provide high-speed telegraphy but also to counter the carpal tunnel syndrome of the day, called "telegrapher's wrist." As opposed to the north/south, up and down tapping motion used with a telegraph key, the bug employed an east/west, back and forth motion between the thumb and index finger.

At the end of the day, I'd usually check with Bill and Cora at the newsstand to see if they had any errands for me. I'd offer to take the garbage to the dump or maybe run some sandwiches across to the bunkhouse for the switch crew, angling for a bottle of my favourite soda pop, Calgary Big Orange, with the famous buffalo logo etched on the glass.

My favourite day around the station was Dad's day off, Sunday. I'd disappear downstairs to hang out in the operator's office with Fergie, the relief operator covering the day shift, or with Bill Timinsky, who came on duty at 4:00 p.m. Sunday was also the day when the operators had to record the serial numbers of all freight and passenger cars in the yard and transmit this data to Calgary Dispatch. This same activity happened at rail yards across the country. The information was compiled by central dispatch in Winnipeg, tracking all CPR and "foreign" rolling stock across Canada.

It became my job to run down to the far east end of the yard and record the car numbers, complete with my own clipboard. I was so proud to have this task that it was years later when I realized I had saved the operators a mile or two of legwork and hours of their time. It was also a couple of hours that I was completely out of their hair!

During my life living and working at the station, communications evolved slowly – unlike the trains and what powered them.

PART III

In the Train Station's Backyard

Left: Life at the station begins. Canadian Pacific station, Banff, 1948.
PHOTOGRAPHER: CANADIAN PACIFIC RAILWAY. COURTESY EXPORAIL AND CANADIAN PACIFIC RAILWAY ARCHIVES, P170-NS-7932_PPP.

Below: Donald Smith driving in the last spike at Craigellachie, November 7, 1885.
PHOTOGRAPHER: CANADIAN PACIFIC. COURTESY WHYTE MUSEUM OF THE CANADIAN ROCKIES, MARY SCHAFFER FONDS, V527/PS-1-810.

Above: William Cornelius Van Horne.
PHOTOGRAPHER UNKNOWN. COURTESY DAVID FLEMING.

Opposite, above: Original Banff Springs Hotel, ca. 1900 – 1910.
PHOTOGRAPHER: BYRON HARMON. COURTESY WHYTE MUSEUM OF THE CANADIAN ROCKIES, BYRON HARMON FONDS, V263-NG-002.

Opposite, below: F.L. "Frank" Gainer, agent, Cochrane, ca. 1918.
COURTESY GAINER FAMILY COLLECTION.

Above: Enid Mary Maggs, Cochrane, 1917.
COURTESY GAINER FAMILY COLLECTION.

Opposite: Gainer family in front of Banff station (sister Mavis missing from photo, teaching in Rocky Mountain House), 1948.
COURTESY GAINER FAMILY COLLECTION.

FLG Terry Enid
Fred Frances Sylvia

Above: My dad (front row, second from right) on his first day on the job in Banff, July 1948.
COURTESY GAINER FAMILY COLLECTION.

Left: A Banff bear on duty, ca. 1940 – 1948.
PHOTOGRAPHER: GEORGE NOBLE. COURTESY WHYTE MUSEUM OF THE CANADIAN ROCKIES, GEORGE NOBLE FONDS, V227-3289.

Opposite: Identical American Flyer electric train to my Christmas raffle win, but wrong kid(!), 1948.
PHOTOGRAPHER UNKNOWN. COURTESY GLENBOW ARCHIVES, IP-13Y-14B.

NEW YORK CENTRA
READING

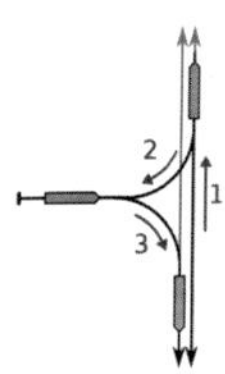

Top: Fred and me on the balcony of Banff station residence, ca. 1949.
COURTESY GAINER FAMILY COLLECTION.

Above: *Canadian Pacific* movie train on set; action shot at Canmore (Rundle Mountain in background), 1948.
PHOTOGRAPHER UNKNOWN. COURTESY GLENBOW ARCHIVES, PA-2453-378.

Right: Diagram of a wye for turning trains.
COURTESY *WIKIPEDIA*.

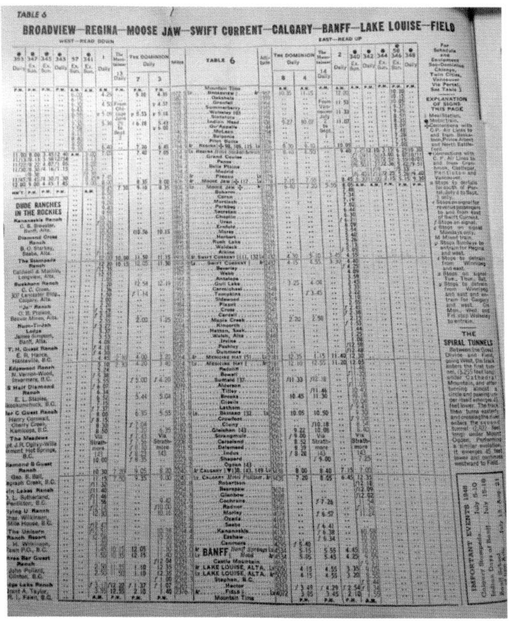

TABLE 6

BROADVIEW—REGINA—MOOSE JAW—SWIFT CURRENT—CALGARY—BANFF—LAKE LOUISE—FIELD

Above: Banff Springs and the Bow Valley, ca. 1930. PHOTOGRAPHER: BYRON HARMON. COURTESY WHYTE MUSEUM OF THE CANADIAN ROCKIES, BYRON HARMON FONDS, V263/NA-3737.

Left: CPR timetable, showing Trains 1, 2, the Dominions and the Mountaineer, 1948. COURTESY STEVE BOYKO.

Opposite, above: Me in front of the original fireplace, Banff station waiting room, 2016.
COURTESY GAINER FAMILY COLLECTION.

Opposite, below: Interior of a colonist class railcar. Although built in the 1890s and early 1900s, colonist cars were still in use through the 1950s, chartered by Fugazy Travel of New York for all-girl teen tours to the Rockies.
COURTESY GLENMORE ARCHIVES, NA-978-4.

Above: 5931, a massive Selkirk 2-10-2 locomotive on display at Heritage Park in Calgary, 2017.
COURTESY GAINER FAMILY COLLECTION.

Left: Palliser Hotel dining room, Calgary, ca. 1940s.
PHOTOGRAPHER: NICHOLAS MORANT. COURTESY WHYTE MUSEUM OF THE CANADIAN ROCKIES, V50-A5-Z-267.

Above: The Dominion at Banff station, 1948.
PHOTOGRAPHER: NICHOLAS MORANT. COURTESY EXPORAIL AND CANADIAN PACIFIC RAILWAY ARCHIVES, P170-M_4045_300PPP.

Below: General Motors test diesel set leading the Dominion, 1949.
COURTESY GAINER FAMILY COLLECTION.

Above: Diesel power on the Dominion at Castle Mountain, 1952.
PHOTOGRAPHER: NICHOLAS MORANT. COURTESY WHYTE MUSEUM OF THE CANADIAN ROCKIES, NICHOLAS MORANT FONDS, V500_62_3_PG129_NS_027.

Below: Morning departure of the Mountaineer, with open-air observation car, 1952.
PHOTOGRAPHER: RON DUKE. COURTESY WHYTE MUSEUM OF THE CANADIAN ROCKIES, RON DUKE FONDS, V180_I.D.A_131_NA_179.

Top: Rare photo of eastbound Mountaineer at Morant's Curve, 1953.
PHOTOGRAPHER: NICHOLAS MORANT. COURTESY WHYTE MUSEUM OF THE CANADIAN ROCKIES, NICHOLAS MORANT FONDS, V50-A5-Z-245.TIF.

Above: Pacific Northwest Circle Tour brochure, 1954.
COURTESY GAINER FAMILY COLLECTION.

Opposite, above: Cartan Tours of Chicago, Canadian Rockies brochure, 1953.
COURTESY GAINER FAMILY COLLECTION.

Opposite, below: Vanderbilt Tours of New York, Canadian Rockies brochure, 1955.
COURTESY GAINER FAMILY COLLECTION.

Forget your daily Cares and come along on Cartan's
CANADIAN ROCKIES WONDERLAND
15 thrilling Days of REST and RELAXATION
DELUXE Accommodations for your COMPLETE Enjoyment
JASPER PARK · COLUMBIA ICEFIELD · LAKE LOUISE · BANFF
CONDENSED ITINERARY
TWIN CITIES
CHICAGO
EVERY FRIDAY:
JUNE 19th to AUGUST 21st, 1953
PERSONALLY CONDUCTED PARTIES OF 40-42

Vanderbilt Better Tours
California
Pacific Northwest
Canadian Rockies
SCENIC TOUR OF THE WEST
VIA THE STREAMLINERS
ESCORTED 14 DAYS
$255 up-plus tax
FEATURING 7 NIGHTS IN HOTELS
SEE MORE ON A VANDERBILT TOUR!

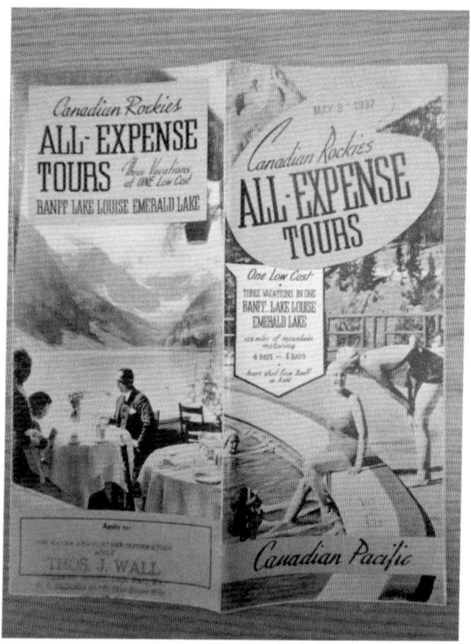

Above: Well-dressed passengers boarding their Pullman on the Mountaineer, ca. 1950.
PHOTOGRAPHER: RON DUKE. COURTESY WHYTE MUSEUM OF THE CANADIAN ROCKIES, RON DUKE FONDS, V180_I.D.A._131_NA_179_1.

Left: Canadian Pacific's Canadian Rockies brochure.
COURTESY GAINER FAMILY COLLECTION.

Opposite: A 1948 Chrysler Deluxe on the Banff Jasper Highway. Real luxury!
PHOTOGRAPHER: GEORGE NOBLE. COURTESY WHYTE MUSEUM OF THE CANADIAN ROCKIES, GEORGE NOBLE FONDS, V227-787.

Above: The Royal Train (King George and Queen Elizabeth) at Field, Engine 2850, 1939.
PHOTOGRAPHER: NICHOLAS MORANT. COURTESY WHYTE MUSEUM OF THE CANADIAN ROCKIES, NICHOLAS MORANT FONDS, V500/A3/57-339-1.

Left: Princess Elizabeth and Philip square dancing in Calgary, 1951.
COURTESY GAINER FAMILY COLLECTION.

Above: Fairholme ranch house, 1958.
COURTESY WHYTE MUSEUM OF THE CANADIAN ROCKIES, V337-PD-1.

Left: "You want me to go where?" Princess Margaret goes to church, 1958.
PHOTOGRAPHER: BILL GIBBONS. COURTESY WHYTE MUSEUM OF THE CANADIAN ROCKIES, BILL GIBBONS FONDS, V-190-1.H-3-NA-03.

Opposite: Dad and Mom all decked out for Princess Margaret's dinner at the Banff Springs Hotel.
COURTESY GAINER FAMILY COLLECTION.

Above: Captain O'Brien-ffrench, Marquis de Castelthomond, ca. 1948 – 1953.
COURTESY WHYTE MUSEUM OF THE CANADIAN ROCKIES, MOORE FAMILY FONDS, V439/NA66-415.

Left: Queen Elizabeth at the Cadet camp, 1959.
COURTESY WHYTE MUSEUM OF THE CANADIAN ROCKIES, V8-ACCN7237.

Opposite, above: Interior shot, sleeping car of the Grey Cup train, 1948. Victorious return to Calgary with Grey Cup.
COURTESY GLENBOW ARCHIVES, PA-2453-378.

Opposite, below: 1958 Grey Cup game, Hamilton vs. Winnipeg.
COURTESY GAINER FAMILY COLLECTION.

Top: Charlie Beil ice carving for the Winter Carnival in front of the Mount Royal Hotel, ca. 1940 – 1948.
PHOTOGRAPHER: BYRON HARMON. COURTESY WHYTE MUSEUM OF THE CANADIAN ROCKIES, BYRON HARMON FONDS, V263-NA-3798.

Above: Banff Winter Carnival ice palace on the Bow River, ca. 1950 – 1954.
PHOTOGRAPHER: GEORGE NOBLE. COURTESY WHYTE MUSEUM OF THE CANADIAN ROCKIES, GEORGE NOBLE FONDS, V227-4732.

Left: The carnival's toboggan slide, from St. Julien Road down Caribou Street to Beaver Street, 1956.
PHOTOGRAPHER: GEORGE NOBLE. COURTESY WHYTE MUSEUM OF THE CANADIAN ROCKIES, GEORGE NOBLE FONDS, V227-4818.

Below: Banff Winter Carnival regatta at the Cave and Basin pool, one of the carnival's most popular events, ca. 1948 – 1958.
PHOTOGRAPHER: GEORGE NOBLE. COURTESY WHYTE MUSEUM OF THE CANADIAN ROCKIES, GEORGE NOBLE FONDS, V227-4724.

Above: Banff Children's Choir awaits arrival of the carnival train, Banff station, 1950.
PHOTOGRAPHER: GEORGE NOBLE. COURTESY WHYTE MUSEUM OF THE CANADIAN ROCKIES, GEORGE NOBLE FONDS, V227-4593.

Left: Princess Patricia's Canadian Light Infantry Band leads carnival parade from station, 1958.
PHOTOGRAPHER: GEORGE NOBLE. COURTESY WHYTE MUSEUM OF THE CANADIAN ROCKIES, GEORGE NOBLE FONDS, V227-4593.

Opposite, above: Carnival train unloading at Banff station, 1958.
COURTESY GLENBOW ARCHIVES, PA-1599-47-17.

Opposite, below: A Brewster Tally-Ho carrying sightseers at the Buffalo Paddock, ca. 1900.
PHOTOGRAPHER: BYRON HARMON. COURTESY WHYTE MUSEUM OF THE CANADIAN ROCKIES, BYRON HARMON FONDS, V263-NA-3711.

Top: Brewster fleet meets the Dominion at Banff station, ca. 1947 – 1950.
PHOTOGRAPHER: GEORGE NOBLE. COURTESY WHYTE MUSEUM OF THE CANADIAN ROCKIES, GEORGE NOBLE FONDS, V227-759.

Above: Rocky Mountain Tours bus and garage, site of today's Grizzly House, ca. 1952.
PHOTOGRAPHER: GEORGE NOBLE. COURTESY WHYTE MUSEUM OF THE CANADIAN ROCKIES, GEORGE NOBLE FONDS, V469-3028.

Above: Brewster "Sky Views" at the Columbia Icefield, ca. 1950.
PHOTOGRAPHER: GEORGE NOBLE. COURTESY WHYTE MUSEUM OF THE CANADIAN ROCKIES, GEORGE NOBLE FONDS, V227-764.

Below: The King Edward Hotel, ca. 1949.
PHOTOGRAPHER: GEORGE NOBLE. COURTESY WHYTE MUSEUM OF THE CANADIAN ROCKIES, GEORGE NOBLE FONDS, V227-2050.

Above: Mount Royal Hotel rotunda, ca. 1920 – 1950.
PHOTOGRAPHER: GEORGE NOBLE. COURTESY WHYTE MUSEUM OF THE CANADIAN ROCKIES, GEORGE NOBLE FONDS, V469/2481.

Below: The Cascade Hotel opens, 1948.
COURTESY WHYTE MUSEUM OF THE CANADIAN ROCKIES, V227-2159.

HALIFAX TRURO & PICTOU MAIL

Opposite, above: The Homestead Hotel, annex and Concord stagecoach, 1952.
PHOTOGRAPHER: DON HARMON. COURTESY WHYTE MUSEUM OF THE CANADIAN ROCKIES, BYRON HARMON FONDS, V263/NA-3463.

Opposite, below: The Gammon Motel, ca. 1956.
PHOTOGRAPHER: GEORGE NOBLE. COURTESY WHYTE MUSEUM OF THE CANADIAN ROCKIES, GEORGE NOBLE FONDS, V469-3387.

Top: Western Electric telegraph key, ca. 1890 – 1920.
COURTESY HAROLD KRAMER.

Above: The "bug" semi-automatic telegraph key, ca. 1920 – 1950.
COURTESY HAROLD KRAMER.

Top: Selkirk 5926 "filling up" at the Banff water tower, 1949.
PHOTOGRAPHER: NICHOLAS MORANT. COURTESY EXPORAIL AND CANADIAN PACIFIC RAILWAY ARCHIVES, P170-M_4045.

Above: The Banff ice house, constructed in 1911 and moved to its present location in 2017, the future site of the Railway Heritage Village.
COURTESY GAINER FAMILY COLLECTION.

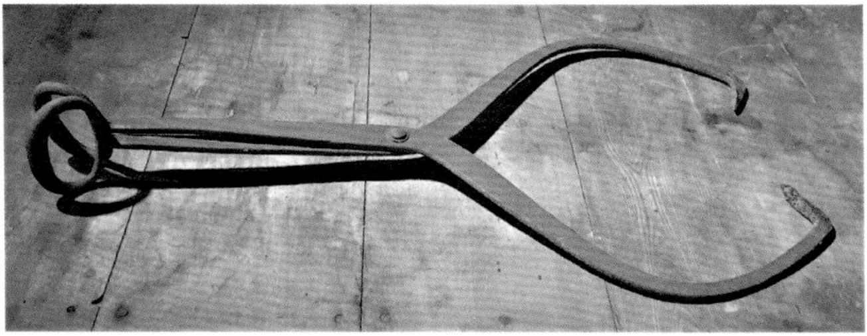

Top: Large ice tongs used to grip ice blocks weighing up to 500 pounds.
COURTESY GAINER FAMILY COLLECTION.

Centre: Large ice chisel used to break up large ice blocks into manageable sizes for iceboxes.
COURTESY GAINER FAMILY COLLECTION.

Left: A speeder on display, Delburne, ca. 1940 – 1970.
COURTESY GAINER FAMILY COLLECTION.

Above: Bull moose at Vermilion Lakes, ca. 1940s. Was this our dinner?
PHOTOGRAPHER: GEORGE NOBLE. COURTESY WHYTE MUSEUM OF THE CANADIAN ROCKIES, GEORGE NOBLE FONDS, V227-3417.

Below: Bob Campbell cutting ice at Lake Louise, ca. 1910 – 1914.
COURTESY WHYTE MUSEUM OF THE CANADIAN ROCKIES, GEORGE PARIS FONDS, V484/NA66-2057.

Above: Engineer and fireman watering a Selkirk locomotive, 1948.
PHOTOGRAPHER UNKNOWN. COURTESY DAVID FLEMING.

Below: Banff's first water tower. A speeder in the foreground, equipped with water pump and hose to put out fires along right-of-way caused by sparks from the steel wheels, ca. 1900 – 1920.
COURTESY WHYTE MUSEUM OF THE CANADIAN ROCKIES, V573-NA-2180.

Opposite, above: Moffatt's farm today, site of the Fenlands Banff Recreation Centre, 2017.
COURTESY GAINER FAMILY COLLECTION.

Opposite, below: The sandhill today, 2017.
COURTESY GAINER FAMILY COLLECTION.

Above: Yours truly all decked out for the Dominion Day Parade, complete with blazer, tie and slacks, 1950.
COURTESY GAINER FAMILY COLLECTION.

Left: Warden Hubert "Beaver" Green, ca. 1940s.
COURTESY WHYTE MUSEUM OF THE CANADIAN ROCKIES, V245-10-PA2.

Above: My monster fish, 1949.
COURTESY GAINER FAMILY COLLECTION.

Above: Whiskey Creek from Marmot Street bridge, 2017. What happened to the water?
COURTESY GAINER FAMILY COLLECTION.

Below: Whiskey Creek at CPR culvert, ca. 1950s.
COURTESY WHYTE MUSEUM OF THE CANADIAN ROCKIES, V488-1-A-NA-118-1.

Opposite, above: Whiskey Creek at the same CPR culvert, 2017. Where did you go?
COURTESY GAINER FAMILY COLLECTION.

Opposite, below: Forty Mile Creek, 2017. Once upon a time, a wetland, now a trench.
COURTESY GAINER FAMILY COLLECTION.

Left: One of many beaver lodges between the three Vermilion Lakes, ca. 1940s.
PHOTOGRAPHER: GEORGE NOBLE. COURTESY WHYTE MUSEUM OF THE CANADIAN ROCKIES, GEORGE NOBLE FONDS, V227-3293.

Below: Moose feeding at Vermilion Lakes, when the Bow Valley was the moose kingdom, ca. 1940s.
COURTESY WHYTE MUSEUM OF THE CANADIAN ROCKIES, A500-A2-07.

SHAMROCK

821. BEAVER

Opposite, above: Fishing the stream connecting First and Second lakes. Lots of water (and fish) in the day, ca. 1930s and 1940s.
COURTESY WHYTE MUSEUM OF THE CANADIAN ROCKIES, V454-NG5-402.

Opposite, below: A Banff beaver.
PHOTOGRAPHER: BYRON HARMON. COURTESY WHYTE MUSEUM OF THE CANADIAN ROCKIES, BYRON HARMON FONDS, V263/NA-2898.

Top: Remnants of the beaver ponds, 2017.
COURTESY GAINER FAMILY COLLECTION.

Above: Here come the '50s. Let the good times roll!
COURTESY GAINER FAMILY COLLECTION.

GRADS

Opposite, above: The Cave and Basin swimming pool, ca. 1950s.
PHOTOGRAPHER: GEORGE NOBLE. COURTESY WHYTE MUSEUM OF THE CANADIAN ROCKIES, GEORGE NOBLE FONDS, V263-NA-3538.

Opposite, below: The amazing Edmonton Grads, ca. 1930s.
PHOTOGRAPHER UNKNOWN. COURTESY JIM ALEXANDER.

Left: Dad's nomination night (left to right: Earl Gammon, Jimmy Simpson Sr., Frank Gainer, Bill Bryant), 1955.
FROM *BANFF CRAG & CANYON*. COURTESY GAINER FAMILY COLLECTION.

Below: Dad's pink Rambler, 1958.
COURTESY GAINER FAMILY COLLECTION.

Left: Train 5, express and mail train, ca. 1950s.
COURTESY GAINER FAMILY COLLECTION.

Below: The Canadian at Castle Mountain, 1955.
PHOTOGRAPHER: NICHOLAS MORANT. COURTESY WHYTE MUSEUM OF THE CANADIAN ROCKIES, NICHOLAS MORANT FONDS, V500-55-56.

Opposite, above: The westbound Canadian arrives in Banff, 1956. Station master kiosk right foreground, Garden Tracks right background, ice house left background.
PHOTOGRAPHER: NICHOLAS MORANT. COURTESY EXPORAIL AND CANADIAN PACIFIC RAILWAY ARCHIVES, P170-M_7446_300PPP.

Opposite, below: The classic Canadian photo at Morant's Curve, ca. 1956.
PHOTOGRAPHER: NICHOLAS MORANT. COURTESY WHYTE MUSEUM OF THE CANADIAN ROCKIES, NICHOLAS MORANT FONDS, V500-54.

Above: A look-alike to Banff's switch engine, ca. 1948 – 1952.
PHOTOGRAPHER: NICHOLAS MORANT. COURTESY WHYTE MUSEUM OF THE CANADIAN ROCKIES, NICHOLAS MORANT FONDS, V500_BL_69_PG75_NS_004.

Below: The newsstand and corridor to the baggage room, ca. 1950s.
PHOTOGRAPHER: GEORGE NOBLE. COURTESY WHYTE MUSEUM OF THE CANADIAN ROCKIES, GEORGE NOBLE FONDS, V263-NA-3447.

Above: Doug Young, Paddy and me, 1950. Note the CP executive car parked on the Willow Tracks in the background.
PHOTOGRAPHER: FRED GAINER. COURTESY GAINER FAMILY COLLECTION.

Left: Operator Alex Leeb preparing train orders, ca. 1958 – 1960.
PHOTOGRAPHER: NICHOLAS MORANT. COURTESY WHYTE MUSEUM OF THE CANADIAN ROCKIES, NICHOLAS MORANT FONDS, V500-A2-R-85-1.

Above: Eastbound Mountaineer labours up Kicking Horse Pass, 1952.
PHOTOGRAPHER: NICHOLAS MORANT. COURTESY WHYTE MUSEUM OF THE CANADIAN ROCKIES, NICHOLAS MORANT FONDS, V500-A2-R-50.

Above: Early season Mountaineer prepares to depart Banff. Note the small baggage car followed by Pullman sleepers.
PHOTOGRAPHER: RON DUKE. COURTESY WHYTE MUSEUM OF THE CANADIAN ROCKIES, RON DUKE FONDS, V180_I.D.A_131_NA_179_3.

Below: CP Express reefer, ca. 1940s and 1950s.
COURTESY GAINER FAMILY COLLECTION.

Above: Full-throttle 5900 leading freight steams into Banff, ca. 1950.
PHOTOGRAPHER UNKNOWN. COURTESY GLENBOW ARCHIVES, PA-4013-1538.

Below: Way freight works, Banff yard, ca. 1940s.
PHOTOGRAPHER UNKNOWN. COURTESY GLENBOW ARCHIVES, PA-4103-179.

Left: Dad at his desk, 1954. PHOTOGRAPHER: FRED GAINER. COURTESY GAINER FAMILY COLLECTION.

Below: 1948 Lincoln Continental. PHOTOGRAPHER UNKNOWN. COURTESY JACKSON-BARRETT AUCTIONS, SCOTTSDALE, AZ.

Above: Nicholas Morant, ca. 1950s.
PHOTOGRAPHER: NICHOLAS MORANT. COURTESY WHYTE MUSEUM OF THE CANADIAN ROCKIES, NICHOLAS MORANT FONDS, V500-B3-3.

Below: Group photo in front of the rock garden, east end of the station, ca. 1950.
PHOTOGRAPHER: GEORGE NOBLE. COURTESY WHYTE MUSEUM OF THE CANADIAN ROCKIES, GEORGE NOBLE FONDS, V227-1277.

Above: John and Muriel Owen's log home on Glen Avenue, Banff, 2018.
COURTESY GAINER FAMILY COLLECTION.

Left: John and Muriel Owen.
PHOTOGRAPHER: JOHN OWEN. COURTESY OWEN FAMILY PERSONAL COLLECTION.

Opposite, above: Summer staff in baggage room office (left to right: Claude Grandbois, Ralph Smith, Ron Thompson, Fred Gainer). Note: rack on left holds destination stamps for checked luggage.
COURTESY GAINER FAMILY COLLECTION.

Opposite, below: A busy photo of the arrival of the eastbound Canadian, 1956. On track 2, to the right, sleepers awaiting the Mountaineer; on the left, the information kiosk and awaiting buses; in the background, express reefers parked for unloading on the Willow Tracks.
PHOTOGRAPHER: NICHOLAS MORANT. COURTESY EXPORAIL AND CANADIAN PACIFIC RAILWAY ARCHIVES, P170-M_6407_300PPP.

Left, above: Baggage boys and redcaps in front of baggage room doors and site of "the quarters game" (left to right: Fred Gainer, John Stuckert, Claude Grandbois, unknown and Spud).
COURTESY GAINER FAMILY COLLECTION.

Left, below: Curly's company, Happiness Tours', brochure, 1948.
COURTESY GAINER FAMILY COLLECTION.

Esso

Opposite, above: Redcap working the Canadian.
PHOTOGRAPHER: NICHOLAS MORANT. COURTESY DAVID FLEMING.

Opposite, below: Me as redcap, sorting luggage off the Canadian.
PHOTOGRAPHER: NICHOLAS MORANT. COURTESY DAVID FLEMING.

Above: Location of switch torn out by boxcar.
COURTESY GAINER FAMILY COLLECTION.

Top: Home sweet home: identical to Jim and Bob's caboose, Heritage Park, Calgary. PHOTOGRAPHER: TERRY GAINER. COURTESY GAINER FAMILY COLLECTION.

Above: Inside a caboose (left to right: Fred Gainer, John Stuckert, Ralph Smith). Note the Heinz box full of Carling's Black Label beer!
PHOTOGRAPHER: CLAUDE GRANDBOIS. COURTESY GAINER FAMILY COLLECTION.

Opposite: Space Needle, Seattle, on the site of the Seattle World's Fair, 1962.
COURTESY SMUGMUG.

Opposite, inset: Great Northern Railroad's Seattle World's Fair advertisement.
COURTESY GAINER FAMILY COLLECTION.

Seattle invites you to wondrous worlds of tomorrow at the Century 21 Exposition...April 21 to October 21
SPACE AGE WORLD'S FAIR
Great Northern invites you to go there...carefree, car-free...in the comfort of its modern streamlined trains
GREAT WAY TO GO to Seattle...Great Northern's great trains: incomparable Empire Builder and the Western Star
CANADA

Canadian Pacific
BY LAND
BY SEA
BY AIR
Canadian Pacific
WORLD'S GREATEST TRAVEL SYSTEM

Opposite: Canadian Pacific poster. Train, ship and Bristol Britannia airplane, ca. 1956 – 1964.
COURTESY GLENMORE ARCHIVES, POSTER 5.

Above: HMS *Canberra*, my home for two weeks, 1962.
COURTESY GAINER FAMILY COLLECTION.

Below: Victor Sugg's rock garden in 2017.
PHOTOGRAPHER: TERRY GAINER. COURTESY GAINER FAMILY COLLECTION.

Above: Willow Tracks, ca. 1940 – 1962, to be restored as part of Railway Heritage Village.
COURTESY EXPORAIL AND CANADIAN PACIFIC RAILWAY ARCHIVES, P170-B_5533_1A_300PPP.

Below: Banff station: back to respectability, 2018.
COURTESY GAINER FAMILY COLLECTION.

THE ICE HOUSE AND THE WATER TOWER

Most people look for my third eye when I talk about the importance of an ice house and a water tower for passenger trains. But without ice, the trains of yesteryear would have been most uncomfortable, and without water they couldn't go anywhere. During the 70-year reign of the steam locomotive, however, water was the key ingredient.

Banff's own ice house had been constructed long ago in 1911 to provide passenger trains and refrigerated express cars with ice for cooling. At that time, the railways of North America had just begun to build the "new" style of heavyweight, steel-sided railcars, furnished with such luxuries as electricity, running water, flush toilets and private sleeping accommodations. After the First World War, passenger rail travel had grown exponentially, ushering in the golden age of rail travel, and the railways of North America waged fierce marketing battles for customers. Customer demand had changed: simple utilitarian transportation from point A to point B was no longer sufficient.

The journey was becoming as important as the destination and a new luxury was introduced: air conditioning. Innovations in railcar construction meant that the passenger cars could be cooled by large fans, powered by direct current (DC) generators that circulated the air through ducts passing over large ice blocks stored in watertight compartments in the chassis underbelly. A three-inch-wide fan belt, running from a pulley attached to the centre of the rotating train axle, powered the DC generators that were also mounted below the undercarriage.

A minimum track speed of about 17 mph generated sufficient electrical current to power the fans as well as electric lighting for the train interiors. When the train was stationary, large DC batteries could power the electrical systems for about two hours before recharging. Air conditioning soon went from a luxury to a must, no longer just a perk for first-class travellers. Even the day coaches were outfitted for ice cooling. This rudimentary technology worked well, but only with a constant supply of ice throughout the summer months.

The Canadian winter provided an inexhaustible and inexpensive source of ice, cut from frozen rivers and lakes all across the country, but storing the ice through the summer months was the challenge. The answer lay in solid, well-insulated structures that became known as "ice houses," positioned in key locations along the rail lines.

Constructed with walls two feet thick, ice houses were filled with sawdust for insulation. The exterior walls were covered in CPR-tartan-red tarpaper that, without close inspection, looked like brick construction. (The traditional CPR colour covered all service buildings owned by the company.) After the ice had been cut and hauled to an ice house, blocks were then rolled in sawdust as an extra layer of insulation and stacked on shelves made with heavy planks and 6 x 6 wooden beams capable of supporting thousands of pounds. Sawdust also impeded the natural process of ice melding together to form larger blocks. Across the top of the building, a 12 x 12 beam not only supported the apex of the roofline but also supported a sliding, block-and-tackle apparatus to lift the ice blocks off a sled or truck bed. In winter, the ice blocks were stacked high on the various levels, and in the summer the process was reversed when the ice was required for cooling. To "ice" the train, crews used large tongs and chisels to manoeuvre the ice blocks onto a cart and into the holding tanks of the railcars.

To service the dining car, a workman would climb an exterior railing onto the roof, positioning himself over the ice chute that dropped down to the icebox in the dining car. Smaller blocks of ice would be chiselled off and then tossed up to him by his co-worker. The ice was released down the chute until the compartment was full. I had watched this masterful performance almost daily during the summer months, and it often drew a crowd of fascinated passengers along the station platform.

For a young boy who spent hours prowling about the train yard, the ice house had always been a place of mystery. Located across the tracks about 220 yards east of the station, the building was connected by a wooden platform laid across five sets of tracks to the main platform. The ice house was always locked, further adding to the intrigue. Whenever I queried this, I'd always get the same answer: once upon a time, a child about my age got locked in an ice house and was found months later frozen solid. But, further adding to the mystery, a curious sequence of incidents occurred when I was 12.

The section foreman of the day, Dad's good friend who shall remain nameless, lived in a house just beyond the rock garden at the east end of the station. On one or two of his visits, the doors into our living room were closed, for "private railroad talk," according to my mother. My young imagination got the best of me one time. The trick of placing a large glass firmly against the closed door with my ear pressed into its mouth worked wonders to magnify the sound, and I heard that they might have to take the speeder out later that night to the Vermilion Lakes to clear a moose off the tracks. If a train hit a moose, it was game over for the moose and a terrible mess.

What a disappointment for me to find out they really seemed to be talking business.

A couple of days later, I was heading into the station bush to play and spotted the ice house door partially open. I crept up to the door and peered in to check things out. As no one appeared to be around, I entered cautiously and, as my eyes adjusted to the light, was stunned by an unexpected sight. Hanging on hooks from the centre beam was the carcass of a huge moose, minus its head, and fully gutted. I scooted out of there as fast as my legs could carry me. Having been forbidden to enter the ice house, I was now dealing with a conundrum. If I mentioned I had seen the moose, it would give away that I had been in there.

A few days later, Dad's section foreman pal dropped in, leaving some large packages tied up in butcher paper. That night, the Gainer family enjoyed a wonderful dinner of moose pot roast. It was my first experience with moose meat and I can still remember the dark, rich-brown gravy served with roasted potatoes and vegetables, my favourite meal to this day. And then the penny dropped. A moose smashed by a train would not be edible; only a few nights had passed since I overheard the conversation between the section foreman and my dad, and suddenly we had an ample supply of moose meat. I knew then it wasn't road/train kill. But discretion is sometimes the better part of valour, and so I said nothing.

After I reached adulthood, long after my dad's retirement from the railway, I confessed how I had eavesdropped and seen the moose hanging in the ice house. Dad smiled and said, "I always suspected you figured it out, Terry, because you had been spotted entering the ice house that morning. I expected you to eventually say something but never thought it would take this long!" That seemed to impress my dad, probably because it was one of the few times as a kid that I kept my mouth shut.

Until the early '50s, supplying ice for the railway was a godsend for many small businesses and local families in the Banff community during the winter months. Every year in late January, Canadian Pacific would issue tenders to harvest the ice, not only to fill the Banff ice house to capacity for summer passenger train requirements but for the Canadian Pacific Hotels across western Canada, as ice was the major component for kitchen refrigeration in the days prior to mechanical air conditioning. At that time of year, the ice on Lake Minnewanka and the Bow River would be a couple of feet thick, the required depth for "good" ice blocks and more than enough to support the weight of the workers, the sleds, the horses, the winches and, eventually, the tractors.

The contract would call for enough ice to fill 700 boxcars and each block could weigh up to 700 pounds. The contractor would employ 40 to 50 men and 20 teams of horses, and the crews could cut and haul enough ice to fill 18 to 20 boxcars per day. The ice harvest was usually about six weeks in duration, providing valuable employment at a time when Banff had few winter jobs and no safety nets such as employment insurance or welfare. The Banff Springs Hotel, a summer-only operation then, provided no employment in the winter and, except for a week in February during the Banff Winter Carnival, there was minimal commercial activity. Even most of the local restaurants closed through the winter, so any opportunity to make a few dollars was welcomed.

Over the years, the contracts were held variously by Brewster Transport or local cartage operators like the Wheatley family and Charlie Harbidge. (Ted Hart's book, *The Brewster Story*, offers an excellent description of Brewster's winter operations, including the ice harvest.)

Across the country, ice houses were located only in major divisional points like Calgary and Vancouver. Banff was unique; while not a divisional point, it was a major stopover destination in the summer where the air-conditioned cars required servicing. (Plus, it was the source for much of CP's ice in the west and it had to be stored.) But every station on the main line had a water tower beside the tracks, and in rural or mountainous areas stand-alone water towers could be found in the middle of nowhere. In fact, when constructing the rail lines across Canada, water towers often appeared before the train stations were built. Prior to the introduction of diesel-electric motive power, all CP locomotives were powered by steam, and water was as important as the coal or oil required to heat the water to produce the steam. Locomotives came in all shapes and sizes, but they all had one thing in common: they needed water. The capacity of most locomotive reservoirs only allowed for a journey of approximately 150 miles.

After arriving in Banff, steam locomotives became my first fascination and I'd often wander up the platform to the head end to watch the fireman and the engineer inspect the locomotive, oiling the pistons and connecting rods. But the main event for me was to watch the fireman work the waterspout. The locomotive stopped adjacent to the water tower and a large hinged spout was lowered into the tender intake and the valve opened. The tower concept provided a rapid gravity flow and the tender would fill with thousands of gallons in minutes.

Many of the early water towers, similar to the first one constructed in Banff, had a large coal and wood stove positioned inside the tower base. During the winters, the stove was kept stoked by the section gangs, providing just enough heat to keep the water from freezing. Prior to oil-fired locomotives, wood and coal sheds were sometimes located beside the water towers. Wood-burning locomotives had been phased out by coal by 1900. Beginning in the 1920s, most locomotives on the CPR main line were converted to oil burners, which were cleaner and required less labour to maintain, but they still required water.

Banff's water tower was located on the south (town) side of the main line, constructed near the current railway crossing at the west end of the station. By 1953, dieselization of all passenger trains meant water towers were becoming redundant. Until the mid-1950s, CP continued to power freight trains with steam engines, but the conversion to diesel was completed by 1958. There was little fanfare when the Bridge and Building Gang arrived on a spring day in 1959, and, like a sneak attack, the tower disappeared. It broke my heart. I loved those huge steam monsters and, against all logic, always hoped there would be a comeback. It was the end of an era.

THE STATION BUSH

What a backyard we had! The locals simply called it the "station bush," and to us it was nature's version of Disneyland. Cross the tracks and you entered a true wilderness, the greatest playground this child could imagine. Moffatt's farm was the entry point, an abandoned dairy that had been operated by Charles and Mary Moffatt, supplying the community with dairy products. In 1911, Charles had leased the CPR land from the railway tracks to Whiskey Creek and west into the grasslands surrounding Vermilion Lakes. In 1938, a devastating fire had engulfed the barn, destroying all the milking equipment. With no insurance, the Moffatts had abandoned the farm. The remaining buildings were removed, but foundations, old car and truck bodies, pipes, wire, bits and pieces of lumber and sheets of galvanized iron were left behind. Instead of being swallowed by nature, these pieces of junk became our treasure and the building materials we used to construct the huts and forts that staked out our territory along Whiskey and Forty Mile creeks.

Unofficially, we also had access to our own herd of horses. In the summer months, Jack Thomas, a local outfitter, pastured his horses at Moffatt's farm, and at the close of the business day we'd hang out at the town stable, hoping we could ride the horses back to the pasture. Most days Jack would oblige; his gruff exterior hid a great fondness for the kids. Jack operated from a location on the corner of Lynx and Wolf streets, now the site of the Banff Park Lodge. I suspect Jack always knew that, on some summer evenings, we'd remove the hobbles from our chosen horses, slip on a halter and off we'd go through the bush, imagining ourselves as railway surveyors discovering the west.

During the 1954 production of *Fort Saskatchewan*, Jack Thomas had the contract to supply livestock for the movie, so I rode horses to the movie set, constructed just off the Minnewanka road above the old Bankhead townsite, and for a couple of days I hung around to watch the filming. As with the movie *Canadian Pacific*, the action shots were a huge disappointment. Alan Ladd, the hero of the iconic movie *Shane*, was a runt – only five feet five inches tall – and in scenes with Shelly Winters he either stood on a box or she would stand in a hole. I couldn't wait to get back to the station bush and the real Wild West!

Across from the station, a sandhill stretched from the railway tracks to Whiskey Creek. Over the years, we tunnelled into the hill, digging caves and trenches as we re-fought all the wars. The tunnels always caved in; the soil was far too sandy. But the fun we had was unending. It was a magical kingdom where we went after school, on weekends and throughout the summer, reliving the lives of famous western explorers, building rafts to sail the creeks and always ready to thwart any invaders.

On the north edge of the farm, Whiskey and Forty Mile creeks merged and this junction became the headquarters for the Station Bush Gang. From the lumber scraps and the rusting metal sheets left behind at Moffatt's farm we built a lookout post on the sandhill, protecting our hut and the rafts we launched in the creeks.

The rafts were constructed of discarded railway ties we salvaged along the tracks. It took maximum effort for a couple of kids to drag the ties around the sandhill to Whiskey Creek, but eventually the mission was accomplished. Six-inch spikes, provided to us by Archie Roth, an employee of Unwin's Lumberyard, secured the cross braces holding the ties together. Unwin's warehouse was next to the tracks at the edge of the bush. Every generation of kids in Banff loved Archie, a guiding light, showing us how to use our tools to avoid chopping off a finger or slicing open a leg.

What sailors we were, often spending as much time in the water as on the raft during our jousting competitions. To win the competition was important; how else could one become Admiral of the Fleet? I seldom won against my new best friend, Mervin Woodworth, the acclaimed leader of our gang. Mervin was also a mechanical genius; he could make and fix anything.

In the summer of 1953, we moved our fort about a mile further up Forty Mile. Successive flooding from years of heavy runoff had formed a small island, about 7 yards wide and 13 yards long, in a wide spot of the creek. We chose this location to be our new headquarters. We'd have to build our castle – but we already had the moat!

We had to have a bridge, too, so we felled a large tree and lopped off the branches to make it passable. Then we set out to do some serious logging. Twelve-year-old lumberjacks made quite the crew: Mervin Woodworth, Bill McKenzie, Garry McCullough, Wayne Vleck, Bobby Brown, Dave Wickson and yours truly attacked the surrounding forest with axes, saws and a can of brown paint. Trees fell fast and furious and we paid little attention to their size. As the walls rose, the lack of uniformity in log size became apparent, but to us it was a thing of beauty. Cutting the notches in the logs posed a challenge, as we hadn't figured out how deep they should be cut. Numerous, uneven gaps resulted, but we solved that problem by stuffing the gaps with moss, mud and grass and then nailing small saplings in between the logs to hold the insulation. It was a rough-looking solution, but it worked. How proud we were, the new pioneers of the west, breaking trail through the mountains.

Next up was the roof. Our minimal building skills dictated a flat roof, and for access we could cut a trap door in the finished roof. Off we went, back to Unwin's to see what we could scrounge, and once again Archie Roth came to the rescue. I think he was quite amused at the prospect of a bunch of kids trying to build a log cabin. Archie offered to come along with us to advise us on building a roof, but I think he was really curious to see what we were doing. His surprise was obvious when he saw our accomplishment. "Tell you what," he said, "if you help me clean up the mess around the compound fence, I'll give you some scrap lumber for the roof, and, if you do a good job, I'll throw in some cedar shingles for the roof." Cleaning up the mess around the fence was an all-day job, but we were rewarded with enough scrap lumber to cover two roofs, plus a bundle of cedar shingles.

Many years later, when I was old enough to go to the Cascade beer parlour, Archie, then working part-time in the tavern, told me he still chuckled about that day. His boss had sent him to the warehouse to clean up the yard and, when he spotted us, he saw his opportunity to ease his workload. But we might have had the last laugh...

The boards turned out to be odd lengths of tongue and groove pine that were slightly stained and relegated to the scrap heap. We figured tongue and groove would be enough to keep the roof from leaking, so we wouldn't need the shingles for the roof. Between the leftover tongue and groove and the shingles, we now had ample material to manufacture an endless supply of weapons. Tongue and groove pine was perfect to fashion the stock for an arrow gun. And we used the cedar shingles to make the arrows; suddenly we had a lifetime supply![4]

Arrows could be quite nasty if you hit something (or someone), but I don't think we understood the ramifications. We had no premeditated design to wound or maim. We were simply prepared to hold the invaders at bay. The invaders? They were the other school gangs that had forts on Tunnel Mountain or in the bush below the Cave and Basin. Kids being kids, occasionally we'd decide to have a battle. It was a game we played with established rules. All battles were booked in advance at school during lunch or recess. Times and dates were set and both sides would have ample time to prepare. Then we'd fly at it. Everyone had their instruments of battle, from wooden swords to slingshots to arrow guns and staple shooters, all wicked enough if you happened to be in the way. But the Station Bush Gang had perfected the arrow gun. It was uncannily accurate, and most opponents would turn and run once they were confronted by our new and improved "hardware." The Station Bush Gang seldom lost.

But every now and again, perhaps to keep us in our place, the

4 *Over the years, I've often had to answer the question, "What the heck is an arrow gun?" Making an arrow gun was not difficult. Made from scrap and a design handed down from older brothers, a yard-long length of grooved pine or cedar served as the stock. The groove provided the guide for the arrow and the trigger mechanism was a wooden clothespin fastened to the stock. At the other end of the stock, a half-inch-wide rubber band cut from an old car inner tube was fastened with a carpet tack. Stretching the rubber band down the length of the stock, you'd insert it into the jaw of the clothespin. Press down on the clothespin and the rubber band released, propelling the arrow toward the target. It was way too simple, and lethal!*

big guys from high school would put the run on us, knocking over our lean-to shelters and forts to remind us they had been the station bush kings before us. But, try as they might, they could never destroy the cabin; it was too solidly built.

The big guys were two and three years ahead of us in school and had loads of fun chasing us through the bush, taking the odd potshot at our retreating butts with their pellet guns. Wayne Ferguson, Jim Davies and Ian Neilson were the usual leaders and the scourge of our gang. One day we decided to stand and engage them near the CPR wye. Running through the bush, Wayne fired off a blind shot from his pump-action pellet gun and at the same moment I stuck my head out from behind a tree. The pellet zapped me on my forehead, just below the hairline, tearing a neat little furrow a couple of inches long. Immediately, Wayne ran over to help me. The wound bled furiously and soaked my T-shirt as I ran up the tracks toward the station, holding Wayne's handkerchief against my head. I made it to the platform as the Mountaineer was departing. It must have been quite a sight: a kid running up the platform, face streaming blood, providing the passengers with one last glimpse of the Wild West!

Mom was in the kitchen as I burst in the door and almost passed out. One of the staff on the platform located Dad. He bolted upstairs, stuck my head under a cold water tap and held me there until the blood flow lessened. After winding a big towel around my head, he drove me to the hospital. I wore those ten stitches like a badge of honour when I returned to school the next day.

The rest of the evening did not go well, especially when Dad got the full story of our gang war. I made it worse by inventing some highly unbelievable story when Wayne had already been to our house apologizing while I was at the hospital. Wayne got the bouquets for honesty and I got the grief for the big lie.

We were not demented, bloodthirsty kids, just a generation born during the Second World War and the Korean War. We had no TV, there was no internet and a family was lucky to have a phone. We created all our own entertainment, most of it healthy and outdoors, fuelled by wild imaginations and an incredible spirit of inventiveness. Our generational game was war. War or its aftermath was constantly on the radio and in the newspapers. The Nuremberg trials were in full swing, the Cold War had ignited and it was an atmosphere filled with conflict. I think we just played "life" as it was happening around us. No serial killers emerged from our mob.

However, there was much more to our lives than the action in the station bush. Banff was a strong community back in the day, with parades and events occurring year-round, including the Banff Winter Carnival, the Intercollegiate Ski Meet and hockey and baseball tournaments. The King & His Court softball team came to Banff every year to play the local all-stars, and the queen's birthday was a celebration rather than just another long weekend. The big event of the summer was the Dominion Day (Canada Day) parade. The bike-decorating contest was the main event, and most local kids participated. First prize was a ten dollar bill, and that was like a million bucks in the 1950s. Yes, we even dressed up for the parade!

ARE YOU STILL WONDERING ABOUT THE CAN OF BROWN PAINT?

We expected big trouble from the wardens if they discovered our lumberjack activities, taboo inside the park. Therefore, we made a plan to conceal the evidence of our logging. It was a simple plan: we'd paint the freshly chopped tree stumps brown to make them look like old tree cuts. No doubt that would fool Warden Green and take the heat off us. Yeah, right, that would "stump" him!

The warden, Hubert Unsworth Green, had been born in England and came to Canada in 1905. For over 30 years he served with the RCMP, and in the late 1930s he moved to Banff, serving the warden service in various roles and eventually as special warden until his retirement in 1956. Warden Green also had a pen name, Tony Lascelles; he wrote many articles on the native wildlife. He was a staunch defender of Parks policy banning hunting within park borders. During the Depression years in the 1930s, this had been a contentious issue as people scrambled to feed their families.

We called him "Beaver Green" because of the beaver hat he wore in winter. He seemed to know well in advance our every move, where we'd be fishing, for instance, and appear out of the woodwork to check up on us. We didn't realize it at the time how much Warden Green cared for the kids of Banff, giving us a nudge now and again, reminding us to toe the line.

Nor were we aware that our log cabin had been the topic of a conversation between Warden Green, Mervin's father and Dad. He explained to our parents that he had no problem with "boys being boys" and chopping down a few trees to build a hut, but he was at the end of his tether with the escalation of our after-school skirmishes. Green went on to say, "These kids are only 12 and 13 years old and already I'm afraid of what they can do to each other." Although our parents were aware of our shenanigans in the station bush, they were completely caught off guard with the news of our more lethal capabilities. Soon after the meeting, our folks collectively lowered the boom and the

Station Bush Gang's activities were severely curtailed, probably a blessing in disguise. As we entered our teenage years, our focus began to change. Mervin and I became avid hikers and our fishing addiction began.

FORTY MILE AND WHISKEY CREEKS

My first fishing experience had been with Dad and Fred at the junction of the Bow and Spray rivers below Bow Falls. I caught a whopper, an eight-inch whitefish, so I was hooked, and luckily Fred was on hand with his Brownie Hawkeye to catch the moment! But most outings with Dad were at Rainy Bay, a couple of miles beyond the Cave and Basin on the Sundance Canyon road. A beaver dam had raised the water level of the bay, and the trout, mainly cutthroat, would school up where the outflow met the river to feed. This was Dad's favourite spot and he often limited out. But then we discovered the fishing in the station bush.

Looking back, it seems unreal that we had such great fishing holes so close to town and just across the tracks from our home at the train station. Whiskey and Forty Mile creeks were healthy, crystal clear and fast flowing into the early '60s. Both were major spawning streams for the connecting waterways, including the Vermilion Lakes and the Bow River. In the spring, the rainbow and cutthroat filled the creeks, and in the early fall the bull and brown trout moved upstream. Following them upstream were the non-native brook trout that had been stocked by Parks Canada as early as the 1930s to create a more vibrant fishery in the park.[5]

5 *Brook trout are such successful spawners that in the right conditions can overpopulate, resulting in thousands of stunted fish that will outcompete native species for food and territory. That has happened in the national park, threatening the east slope cutthroat. (In recent years, Parks Canada has initiated campaigns to remove the non-native species.)*

At this time, Whiskey Creek flowed west from the Indian Grounds and meandered through a thick forest between the railway tracks and Cougar Street. One of the best fishing holes along the creek was a deep pool directly across the street from Warden Green's home on the south side of Cougar, which pretty much ensured we played by the rules while fishing there. An undermined bank had been carved by the creek, leaving a gravel bed of small smooth stones. Feeding the pool was a stretch of tumbling rapids creating a perfect resting spot for the wary trout.

From Cougar Street, the creek then flowed under the rail line behind the current site of the Banff Park Church, meandering through the station bush in a series of loops and curves, with more steep undermined banks and pools. Whiskey Creek finally joined a turbulent Forty Mile Creek behind the current recreation centre. The merged creeks flowed under the Norquay road, meeting the outflow creek from the Vermilion Lakes. At this point, it became Echo Creek, flowing into the Bow River at "The Point," the locals' name for the meeting of the waters (the canoe dock's current location).

Forty Mile Creek begins at Forty Mile Summit, fed by many outlet streams including Sawback and Mystic Lakes, flowing south into the Bow Valley between Stoney Squaw and Cascade mountains. Until construction began for the Trans-Canada Highway in the early '50s, Forty Mile Creek flowed through a grassy marsh, dividing into many channels, directly in the path of the highway's route. Although an important wetland, the marsh was perceived as an obstacle, so it was eliminated. The construction crew buried the marsh under tons of fill and gouged a channel downstream for about a mile, ensuring the flow would not be impeded, preventing flooding during the highway construction. To cut this channel, a swath of trees and a stretch of sandy, gravelly rapids connecting pools of slow-moving water were removed, leaving a visible scar.

Fortunately, the remainder of Forty Mile Creek was not altered from this point to the junction with Whiskey Creek. It was good fishing, but not without a challenge. Fast water, undermined banks, fallen trees and waterlogged stumps gave the fish excellent habitat. I loved fishing the creeks but spent much of those days getting snagged and losing tackle.

Throughout the summer months, the catch was mostly small brook trout, but come spring and fall the fishing was exceptional as the rainbow and bull trout came out of the Bow River and the Vermilion Lakes to spawn. That was Beaver Green's busy time of year; he had to be vigilant to ensure that fishermen didn't exceed bag limits or snag with three-prong hooks. A lot of Banffites fished in those days, and everyone knew when the fish were running.

Local lore claimed, however, that the real fishing "nirvana" was in the reservoir behind the dam on Forty Mile Creek, which was also Banff's water supply. After the construction of the dam in the 1920s, Parks closed the Forty Mile watershed to hikers and fishermen alike. You weren't even allowed to hike up to the dam. But, for Mervin and me, fishing in the reservoir became our number one challenge in the summer of 1954. Now 13, we were emboldened teenagers on a mission.

Fishing behind the dam wasn't entirely out of bounds. Apparently, certain parks officials and special visitors were often treated to this luxury. Although denied, it was public knowledge that every Labour Day Weekend a certain park superintendent (who shall remain nameless) would take dignitaries and pals on a fishing trip up to the headwaters. The officials in the "Kremlin" (as we locals called the Parks administration building) assumed they would never sully the town water supply like we, the "great unwashed," would surely do, hence the special dispensation. The outing was on horseback, past the reservoir and followed Forty Mile Creek to the headwaters at Sawback Lake. Tales from this annual fishing expedition were legion, with the fish of biblical quantities.

It was no easy task to get beyond the dam: "No Admittance" and "No Trespassing" notices were posted everywhere. The water plant managers and employees were vigilant, and the road from town passed through the government compound where the intentions of young boys with fishing poles might be suspect. Plan A was instituted. We'd simply skirt the dam by climbing up the slope of Stoney Squaw on the west side of the creek, then drop down to the reservoir upstream from the dam, out of view of the water plant. But plan A almost ended in disaster as we began our descent. We had no idea that this shoulder of Stoney Squaw became a steep canyon wall straight down into the reservoir. Had it not been for some scrub pine that I clutched and Mervin's manoeuvres to pull me back, I may have ended up at best the subject of a very cold dunking, or possibly worse. My near miss was quickly forgotten, and we went back to the drawing board in our quest.

The solution was hiding in plain sight. After observing the activity around the compound and the water treatment plant, we realized the government workers did not arrive before 7:00 a.m., so we rode our bikes through the compound at 6:00 a.m., up the fire road and past the water plant and never saw a soul. Though not as advertised by local lore, the fishing was good; we easily limited out, but all the fish were stunted brookies and cutthroat. We were careful not to return to town until early evening, after the plant employees had left for the day. Over the years, we only made two return trips to the reservoir. The risk/reward factor was not in our favour and we kept our "discovery" a secret for years.

Not only was the water quality in the creeks and streams in the 1940s through the early 1960s close to pristine, but so too were the surrounding forests. I'd meet Mervin most mornings when we went fishing at the culvert where Whiskey Creek flowed under the railway tracks. I'd walk about a half-mile east of the station along the tracks, and Mervin had a three-block walk from his home on the corner of Moose and Marten streets. Then we'd fish upstream, sometimes for a couple of miles. No homes existed on the north side of Cougar Street, and Whiskey Creek meandered through heavy woodlands all the way to the old Indian Grounds. It was pure wilderness; a wildlife corridor with swamps, waterfowl and animal life.

The housing construction on the north side of Cougar Street didn't start until the early 1960s, but it happened fast. From the station we could hear the scream of chainsaws being fired up and the rumble of bulldozers as the dense pine forest was flattened. Once cleared, an unsightly trench was gouged behind the boundary of the development (visible today behind the Banff Park Church) to the culvert under the railway tracks, and the original creek bed was buried under tons of landfill. In just a few days of construction, one of the best spawning streams in the Bow Valley was gone.

THE CHANGING ECOSYSTEM

Prior to the coming of the railway, the Vermilion Lakes area had been a huge backwater for the Bow River, flooding the valley during high water in the spring and early summer, creating three lakes and a huge wetland. The construction of the CP rail line in 1883 had proceeded west from Siding 29 (at the base of Cascade Mountain), through the Bow Valley toward Lake Louise. From the crossing of Echo Creek, for the next four miles, the rail line paralleled the riverbank, creating an earthen dam impeding the flow of water across the valley. To balance the water level on each side of the line, culverts were strategically placed, and this created new boundaries for the Vermilion Lakes. The lakes were connected by a network of canals created by nature's own dam builders, beavers that thrived on the willows and aspen trees growing in the wetlands. This sprawling area of water, swamp, streams and ponds was a diverse ecosystem, attracting all kinds of aquatic animals, birdlife and insects, as well as supporting a thriving fishery.

At school, I had met another keen fisherman, George, son of Gus Baracos who owned the Banff Café. Mr. Baracos was a famous personality on the Banff scene and most evenings could be found playing his mandolin and entertaining his guests while they dined. More importantly to me, George's older brother Andrew was a fly-fishing maestro and knew all the tricks about fishing the Vermilion Lakes. Andrew was home from university for the summer and one day agreed to take us fishing.

We crossed the railroad bridge over Echo Creek and then

slogged through swamp and bush, finally reaching the outlet stream from First Lake. And there it was – the biggest beaver dam I have ever seen. We climbed up on the beaver dam and, looking down into a crystal-clear pool, saw so many fish that we could not see the bottom. Hundreds were schooling up, as if awaiting some signal to breech the dam and begin the migration to the spawning beds up Forty Mile and Whiskey creeks. Because a beaver dam is porous, the fish could easily pass through into the creeks and, twice a year, in spring and fall, every deep bend and undermined creek bank with a gravel bottom was thick with spawners.

The channel behind the dam was at least three yards deep and backed up about 55 yards. These were the bull and brook trout that spawned in late summer and early autumn. I later learned the same activity occurred every spring when the rainbow and cutthroat began their spawning exodus. The fishing was too easy: in went the lines and out came the fish. Although the dam was only a couple of miles from town, it attracted few other fishermen; it was tough to access unless you were prepared to slop through heavy brush and swamp like us.

Andrew introduced us to all his favourite spots, including the beaver ponds between Second and Third lakes and the beaver dam on the west shore of Third Lake. To fish the lakes successfully, you needed to fly-fish, so Andrew and George patiently introduced me to the art and we often practised in their backyard on the corner of Wolf and Marten Street. Initially, I thought fly-fishing was simply an exercise to foul your line and snag your flies in the brush, but slowly I became proficient enough to cast a line. The regulars we'd see almost daily included multi-talented fishing guide Les Zarkos, restaurateur and Banff store owner who loved the Vermilion fishery; Jimmy

Shaw with the guiding service at the Banff Springs, who would often be on Second or Third lakes in a rowboat with clients; and Art Krowchuk, a Banff local and hockey star with his own guiding service. I was convinced Art could have caught a fish in a mud puddle; he sure knew how to catch them in Vermilion Lakes. The fish were not the 8- to 10-inch "minnows" you might catch today; they were 14- to 18-inch bull trout and rainbows. Because of the clear, deep water (thanks to the beaver dams' purifying effect), the fish were healthy, not full of worms and parasites like the stunted fish in the Vermilion Lakes today. It was an efficient ecosystem.

In the mid-1950s, I witnessed the "perfect storm" of mostly man-inspired changes to Vermilion Lakes that hastened not only the decline of the fishery but other wildlife too. The Vermilion Lakes have always been a favourite spot for tourists. The setting, with Mount Rundle in the background, has long been a Canadian Rockies icon. As soon as the old highway was opened along the shores of Vermilion Lakes, Brewster and Rocky Mountain Tours offered their own versions of a twilight drive to view the park animal life. This tour was a top-seller because you always saw wildlife. First stop was the town dump, where visitors would be guaranteed to see bears, sometimes a dozen feeding at a time. But the highlight was the Vermilion Lakes and the beaver ponds. The sedge and grassy environment attracted a large moose population, the largest animal in Banff National Park. Moose populated the entire Vermilion Lakes ecosystem then, so it was no trick to view them. The moose obliged night after night, feeding in the wetland, gorging on underwater plants, bulbs and root systems.

Mule deer wandered down off the slopes, feeding on the abundant grasses, and Rocky Mountain sheep inhabited the rock cuts above the road. The ponds were full of beaver and muskrat. A viewpoint at the main beaver pond, about halfway between Second and Third lakes, offered a premier location to watch the beaver at work, as they shored up their dams to keep the water levels high, securing the safety of their beaver lodges and minimizing the distance from the water's edge to the food supply, mainly the willows, aspen and bushes surrounding the ponds. This was classic beaver and muskrat terrain, and the water level maintained the food supply for the moose population that dominated the Bow Valley until the late 1950s. And then they all disappeared.

When our family first arrived in Banff in 1948, we rarely saw an elk; moose dominated the Bow Valley. Severe winters, deep snow and wolves had decimated the elk population of the park. To bolster the stock, Parks Canada imported a small herd from Yellowstone National Park. These elk would have struggled to survive, but with a rabies scare throughout the province, Alberta Fish and Game, supported by Parks Canada, instituted a campaign to eradicate wolves and coyotes as a preventative measure. In Banff and most of Jasper national parks, the wardens successfully eliminated the wolf population. The unintended consequence was a significant increase in the elk population. Over the next few years, the elk population steadily increased to encroach on the townsite, especially during the fall rut. By the late 1950s, the elk population exploded into the Bow Valley as major competitors to other grazers and browsers for the food supply.

The second part of the perfect storm to hit the Bow Valley was the failure of the beaver habitat. Beaver usually migrate to new territory when they need to take longer trips out of the water to access their food. However, in the case of the Vermilion watershed, the migration did not occur because of diminishing food supply but because the water level of the Vermilion Lakes system fell drastically when the wardens dynamited the large beaver dam. Under the beaver dam, an old weir, which had been constructed sometime in the 1930s to help keep the water level constant, was removed as well. In a few days, the water level dropped over three feet; the canoe docks were left high and dry, the beaver canals drained and the streams connecting the beaver ponds were reduced to a trickle. It was the beginning of the end of the Vermilion wetlands as we knew it in the 1950s.

The weir had long been contentious: when the dams were dynamited, and the weir removed, the drastic drop in the water level threatened William Mather's canoe rental business. Mather owned Bow River and Lake Minnewanka Boat Cruises and the canoe rental concession on the Bow River and Vermilion Lakes. Apparently facing legal action from Mather, the Parks Service attempted to restore the water level by rebuilding the weir. Unfortunately, the new weir was not put in place until the following summer, too late to save the beaver population. They had to move on or become victim to the predators when the water level fell.

As I recall, the decision to remove the beaver dams was based on the premise that the ever-increasing water level would threaten the old highway (current Vermilion Lakes Drive) until such a time that the Trans-Canada, which was then under construction high above the lakeshore, would be completed.

The declining water levels began to affect the health of the Vermilion Lakes fishery. The changes were gradual, but throughout the following year we noticed the numbers, size and quality of the catch declined, creating a domino effect on the fishery in Forty Mile and Whiskey creeks. The spawning activity fell off and the shallower water levels in the lakes and beaver ponds over the winter resulted in an ice cover that froze close to the bottom, killing off fish through deprivation of oxygen. At the time, so-called Parks Canada experts declared this was a good thing; Vermilion Lakes would return to a "natural state." The assumption must have been that beaver activity in a wetland in a national park was not natural.

In a few short years, we watched as the Bow Valley underwent a major ecosystem change. The eradication of the wolves begat the explosion of the elk population, the drastic decrease in water levels caused the exit of the beaver colonies and the slow decline of the fishery all came to a head by the mid-1960s.

The lush grasslands that grew in and around the declining lakeshores became a favourite grazing area for the elk, overwhelming the food supply and pushing the moose out of the valley. The dominant ungulates that had ruled the Bow Valley for more than a century were gone and, by 1970, had almost disappeared in Banff National Park.[6]

6 *The beaver did attempt a comeback in the early 1990s. Over the intervening years since the 1960s, the willows, aspen, cottonwoods and birch had grown thick, crowding along the shrunken shoreline of the lakes. In the spring of 1992, while walking the Fenland Trail with a friend, we were excited to see that beaver had cut down several large trees along the bank of Forty Mile Creek, a couple of which were large pine trees. I had never witnessed a pine tree cut down by beaver so assumed these large trees were meant to anchor a large dam across swift-flowing Forty Mile Creek. Two smaller beaver dams had already been constructed on the exit stream from First Lake and the lake level was rising. But Parks rode to the rescue of Vermilion Lakes Drive, removing the beaver dams and relocating the beaver. Once again, nature had been denied.*

PART IV

The Glory Years 1955 – 1962: I've Been Working on the Railroad ...

FABULOUS '50S

The '50s were some of the best years of my life, but there were some big bumps. Like the changing ecosystem in the Bow Valley, the town and the railway were on the cusp of significant upheaval as well, but, in late 1954, my 12-year-old world was shaken to the core when Dad announced he was retiring from CPR. He had already dodged the retirement age of 65, granted a two-year, good-health extension, but age 67 was the upper limit. I had never even entertained the idea that one day we'd have to move away from my kingdom at the station. It didn't matter that we were only moving a few blocks; it was like moving to another world.

In a way, it was. Life at the station was an atypical environment. All I had to do was venture downstairs and there it was, the station community, with its patented lifestyle and unique cast of players. I would miss the proximity and belonging. It now felt like my "Banff the Beautiful" was coming to an end.

In December, we relocated to a two-bedroom duplex at 332 Banff Avenue. It was much smaller than our home at the train station; it didn't have the huge basement and furnace room where my brother and I had our model railroad. I could no longer wander downstairs in the evening to the telegraph office, sending telegrams and practising Morse code, nor could I visit with the station employees whom I had taken for granted. There was little I liked about our new residence.

Thankfully, life on Banff Avenue was short-lived. In June 1955, we moved to 136 Otter Street, a four-bedroom house owned and beside the Christou family, and, with that move, our family began a second phase of life in Banff. It wasn't like returning to the station, but I was excited. The Christous had three children: Tina, George and Jimmy. Tina and my sister Frances had been high school friends and had moved on to city life. Even prior to the move, George and Fred had been best friends and I had known Jim since I started school in Banff. Jim was a year ahead of me in school, and as a rule you generally didn't kick around with younger kids then. But, as neighbours, Jim and I became instant buddies and most days, especially in winter, we could be found in the Christou rumpus room, continually playing the world championship in Ping-Pong. Our parents were close too. Frank and Dad were curling buddies and fellow Rotarians, and he would become a staunch supporter of Dad's through his next, political, career. Mom and Mrs. Christou had much in common. They enjoyed long walks together, volunteered together at the hospital, and rolling bandages in the United Church hall for the Red Cross and morning coffee or afternoon tea was a regular part of their day.

Otter Street was full of kids our age. The Waterhouse family lived two doors down and the McCullough family lived next door to them. In the winter, the Waterhouse backyard became a skating ring where Ronnie and Kenny Waterhouse, Garry McCullough, Jimmy Christou and I replayed the Stanley Cup every night after school. We played for hours under a yard light and it was a lot more fun than the new black and white – and snowy – TV. The Standish family lived just two blocks away on Beaver Street, and in the summer the vacant lot beside their house was the scene of the ongoing game of kick the can. Every evening the whole neighbourhood, regardless of age, joined in. We created our own fun, played hard and were better off for it.

Kick the can was easily the favourite game. All we needed was a can and a yard full of kids for unending entertainment.

Summer mornings would find us congregated at the Cave and Basin. That was back in the days when there was water in the pools instead of concrete, with one pool for swimming and the hot pool for bathing.

That same summer, I met Jim Alexander, a new kid in town who became another lifelong friend. Harry and Helen and their sons Jim and Keith had arrived in the spring of 1955. Mr. Alexander opened a gift and souvenir shop (later to become Pinky's Laundromat) on Wolf Street in between the Modern Restaurant (now Magpie and Stump) and Monod & Medic Ski Shop. I met Jim one evening while playing kick the can. An excellent all-round athlete, he played hockey fast and furious, as if he was seven feet tall, having inherited his mom's athletic genes.

His mom, Helen (Northup) Alexander, had been a star basketball player with the Edmonton Grads, the most famous and successful team to ever represent Canada at any level. The Edmonton Grads was a local team started by high school gym teacher J. Percy Page, and from such humble beginnings it went on to rule the ladies' basketball world. Their record was unbelievable.

Helen's favourite story from her playing days happened during the 1936 Olympics in Berlin. On a day off, the team members were scheduled for a bus tour, but, instead, a huge convertible touring car roared up to the bus stop and a well-dressed young man hopped out. In reasonable English, he told them it was their car that day and off they went, for a tour and a spectacular lunch. The Grads' fame had preceded them! It turned out the young man was of considerable privilege; his name was Vittorio

Mussolini, the dashing 20-year-old son of the Italian dictator, "Il Duce" Benito Mussolini.

Our move to Otter Street coincided with a year of transformation for our family, especially Mom and Dad. With all of the children almost out of the nest, the world became their oyster. Newly retired, Dad entered the political arena, running for MLA for the Banff-Cochrane constituency.

In the 1950s, the Social Credit Party, a blend of conservatism and Pentecostal Christianity, had ruled the Alberta legislature since the 1930s. Dad secured the backing of the local Liberal and Conservative associations, unifying the anti-Social Credit vote and, against all odds (and the pundits), went on to win three consecutive elections until he retired in 1967, just after his 80th birthday. Mom was always his most able campaigner, accompanying him as they knocked on every door in the constituency.

Dad labelled himself a coalition candidate and in his second term split the leader of the opposition portfolio with a Conservative MLA and a Liberal MLA because they were the only three opposition members elected in an otherwise Social Credit landslide. What fun he had, since the opposition in the Alberta legislature is by law allocated 50 per cent of the speaking time! He liked to say that he threw more barbs at the government of the day than you'd find in a basket of fishhooks. Dad was re-energized; he had never wanted to retire. Mom accompanied Dad to Edmonton when the legislature was sitting, and she blossomed in her new role as a politician's wife. (And, as we kids contended, his best advisor.) With the move into politics, they met scores of wonderful new people and embraced their new role in public life.

After the election, as our 1949 Ford began to falter, Dad decided to buy a new car, so he had Fred accompany him to

Calgary to visit the dealerships. Fred took great delight in telling this story. "We must have visited every car dealer in Calgary that day while Dad played his game, exposing a wad of cash to all attending salesmen. After considerable bargaining and offering considerable peeks at his bankroll, he'd head for the door, declaring their cars were too expensive." Fred figured when Dad was finished having fun, they'd end up back at the Ford dealership, make the deal and head for Banff. That was not to be. A slick salesman at American Motors offered a big discount if Dad would take a new deluxe Rambler, but there was a catch. It was pink and white, with a charcoal and pink interior. But it was brand new, with lots of toys and heavily discounted. Dad could not refuse a bargain, in any colour, and made the purchase.

When Dad and Fred arrived in Banff, Mom happened to be in the backyard as the pink apparition entered the driveway. She quickly approached the car, intending to tell the occupants that this was private property and to please "move your car."

"Enid, it's me, Leo. I bought you a new car. I thought you'd like a pink one." But Mom was nobody's fool. Bought *her* a new car? She hadn't driven in years! But she never let on she didn't like it, despite the fact a pink car in the '50s was like a siren and quickly became famous in small-town Banff. "There go the Gainers!" Perhaps Dad had bought the pink monstrosity to ensure he was recognized as he cruised down Banff Avenue.

All our lives changed that year. My sister Frances had left home for university, Fred was in Grade 12 and would be off to college the next year and, much to the chagrin of my parents, I had become a teenager. The know-it-all syndrome had kicked in and, combined with an interest in cars and girls, displaced rafts and Whiskey Creek.

But, most satisfying, I was finally old enough to apply for

full-time summer jobs. The paper route and part-time jobs were behind me. Most school kids in Banff had at least one summer job and sometimes two. We wanted to save for a scooter, a car or even university as the concepts of weekly allowance and student loans had yet to be invented. We knew most of the potential employers (and they surely knew all about us) giving us first crack at the job market. Dad was a good friend of Colin McCartney, the general manager of the Banff Springs, so he could have helped me with employment opportunities there as he had for my sister Frances a couple of years earlier. But I didn't want to work at the Banff Springs and rejected any overtures of help. I was fiercely committed to finding a job on my own. I wanted to work at a gas station with my friend Mervin – at least until the following summer when I'd be old enough to apply for a job with the railway.

Frank Douglas owned the Cascade Esso, located on the corner of Banff Avenue and Elk Street, directly across the street from the school. For the summer of 1956, he hired us as pump jockeys. He was one of the best employers I ever had. He was fair and understood teenagers. Discipline meant a session in his office instead of shouting or humiliation in front of your peers. If you performed the job well, you received the appropriate recognition. In hindsight, I think Mr. Douglas was far ahead of his time.

Companies operating under the Esso banner had to comply with the company's high standard of customer service. Esso had inspectors on the road checking the service stations on a regular basis. These silent shoppers conducted random visits, grading employee performance, cleanliness of the pumps, product displays, the outside facilities, cleanliness of the washrooms and adherence to dress codes. We were proud of our spiffy Esso uniforms and felt incentive to provide our customers with the trademarked Esso Circle Service. Should your customer turn out to be a silent shopper, and you had fully completed the Circle Service checks, you would automatically win five silver dollars, a substantial reward in 1956. On the flip side, if you messed up, your employer was immediately notified and your future as a pump jockey could be in jeopardy.

Cascade Esso provided an unexpected benefit for a teenager. Strategically located on Banff Avenue at the foot of the business district, it was an excellent corner location to observe the foot traffic passing into town. While cleaning and polishing the gas pumps and oil displays, we could tease, ogle and flirt with the girls as they strolled by, ushering in a whole new world of discovery.

CHANGE AND INNOVATION: A REVOLUTION ON THE RAILS

But the biggest change for me in the '50s was CP's announcement in early 1954 regarding a major restructuring of the long-haul passenger train services. The company acted swiftly and in late 1954 amalgamated the Dominions into one train. Separate Dominions continued to leave from Montreal and Toronto but joined together in Sudbury as one train to Vancouver, often over 18 cars in length. Then, in the spring of 1955, Trains 1 and 2, the workhorses of the fleet, were discontinued and the passenger service was shifted to the Dominion, providing frequent stops by means of a "flag" service: if a small station had passengers booked, the train was then flagged for boarding. If there were no passengers waiting, a stop was not required. Trains 5 and 6 were introduced as dedicated express and mail trains to fill the gap after discontinuing the workhorses. Because the length of a passenger train was set at 22 cars to comply with government braking and safety regulations, this in part was the rationale for introducing Trains 5 and 6. While the mail and express functions could have been off-loaded onto the Dominion, seven or eight mail and express cars would severely diminish the number of passenger cars the Dominion could haul, limiting capacity and thereby passenger revenue.

Trains 5 and 6 provided daily service from Fort William to Vancouver and had to qualify as passenger trains due to federal regulations. To comply, CP included a day coach in the consist of seven to ten mail and reefer cars, thereby offering point-to-point passenger service. Usually, they were non-air-conditioned coaches with no amenities or food service and checked luggage service was unavailable. The message was loud and clear: you can ride if you must, but we are an express and mail train. Trains 5 and 6 were the new "all stops" trains, connecting to their counterpart Trains 9 and 10 operating from Fort William to Montreal or Toronto.

The cancellation of the workhorses had a significant impact on the Banff community, as both the morning train service to Calgary and the late evening return no longer existed. It killed the Banff to Calgary train traffic, as both the eastbound Canadian and Dominion were afternoon departures. Banff residents shifted to the local Greyhound service, departing for Calgary at 9:00 a.m., with afternoon and early evening departures back to Banff. In the 1950s and 1960s, the Greyhound depot in Calgary was in the downtown core, near the Hudson's Bay and Eaton's department stores. Fewer passengers, including the Gainers, were taking the train to Calgary.

But the biggest transformation came with the announcement of an all-new train christened the Canadian. Canadian Pacific had made the decision to enter the era of the streamliner, placing the largest order (in 1953) that the Budd Railcar Company would ever receive, a grand total of 173 stainless steel streamliner cars. The 13 complete train sets included scenic dome sleepers, Skyline dome/cafe cars, bedroom and roomette sleepers, drawing room and compartment sleepers, day-nighter coaches, elegant dining cars and baggage-crew dormitories, a total of 18 cars. CP also refurbished 22 heavyweights with stainless steel cladding as tourist sleepers, all with 14 sections of upper and lower berths. The latest FP-9 locomotives were ordered from General Motors, augmenting the existing fleet of FP-7s. These were the preferred locomotives for passenger service, not only because of their attractive streamlined styling but because these locomotives included the heated water reservoirs required to make steam heat for the passenger cars.

Canadian Pacific was launching North America's premier transcontinental train as a valiant attempt to fight the airlines for dominancy in the long-haul travel business. And the Canadian was about to become an icon, synonymous with the best train and rail journey in the world.

The Canadian commenced operations on April 24, 1955, departing simultaneously from Montreal and Toronto, joining together as one train in Sudbury for the cross-country journey to Vancouver. Two days later, at 2:50 p.m., the Canadian arrived in Banff, where a huge crowd had gathered, including Dad and me, to view this magnificent train. As the train glided quietly into the station you could have heard a pin drop. Then the crowd suddenly broke into a huge cheer and the applause was deafening, sending shivers down my spine. Looking up at the sleeping car porter in the car that stopped directly in front of us, I saw tears streaming down his face and he was applauding too. I've never witnessed such group emotion – and all about a train! It was as if the home team had just scored in overtime to win the Stanley Cup. And the enthusiasm continued throughout that first summer of operation. Every day there were as many people at the station to greet the Canadian as there were passengers.

The Canadian was a visual masterpiece. Sleek and stylish, the train sets were considered hallmarks of 20th-century railway design. The streamliner dome cars were hugely popular and gave new meaning to sightseeing on the rails. The Canadian seemed impossibly long; at 18 to 20 cars, it was almost double the length of its steam-era predecessors. Platform extensions were required at many stops; in Banff, the platform had to be extended 200 feet.

The sleek new railcars of the Canadian were the envy of the industry. Led by the attractive streamlined GM locomotives, even the baggage and crew dormitory cars were sleek and new. The tourist sleepers were rebuilt heavyweights and they, too, were clad in gleaming stainless steel, housing 14 sections of upper and lower berths. Two all-new, deluxe, day-nighter coaches followed the tourist sleepers and connected to the Skyline dome cafe car. At least one deluxe dining car led the first-class accommodations, a mix of Manor and Chateau cars followed by a sparkling Park observation dome car. In the height of the season, it was not unusual for an extra tourist sleeper, a second Skyline dome cafe car, a second diner and two or three first-class sleepers to be added to meet demand. The Canadian was an overnight success, catching the imagination of travellers from around the world and becoming the toast of the industry.

In railway jargon, the stainless steel cars of the Canadian were called lightweights, since the construction materials differed significantly from the older, heavyweight, steel-cladded cars. Heavyweights were built with wooden frames clad in riveted steel, with interiors finished in ornate hardwoods. Six-wheel trucks were required at each end of the car to carry the extra weight and to provide a smooth ride. By contrast, the lightweight cars were introduced in the 1930s when refinements in steel processing made stronger stainless steel studs, lighter siding and four-wheeled trucks. The lighter weight was a significant contribution to fuel efficiency.

The Canadian was now CP's premier train service, but the Dominion continued to have one advantage. Since its inception in 1932, the timetable had been set to highlight the Canadian

Rockies from Banff through to Revelstoke in daylight. From a tourist point of view, the westbound Dominion had a schedule superior to the Canadian through the Rockies. The 1955 timetable had the Dominion leaving Banff at 10:20 a.m., completing the passage through the Rockies to Revelstoke by 5:00 p.m., which meant full daylight in all seasons. The Canadian also had daylight passage in the summer months, leaving Banff at 3:10 p.m., and arriving in Revelstoke at 8:30 p.m. But during the fall, winter and early spring, with the sun setting in mid-afternoon, part of the passage was in the dark.

With the introduction of the Canadian, I was even more determined to secure my dream job at the station when I turned 15, CP's minimum age. Over the winter of 1956, I made frequent visits to see Merle, the baggage master, and Walter, the station agent, dropping hints about a job in the baggage room.

A SUMMER DAY AT THE STATION

To spend even a day at the Banff station in the 1950s was a train enthusiast's dream. Passenger trains, freight trains, express trains and mail trains rolled through day and night. We even had our own steam locomotive assigned to Banff for the summer, shunting express and freight cars to the sidings to unload the goods for Banff or to switch coaches and sleeping cars on and off the passenger trains.

The Banff station was the mother ship, the hub for everything that funnelled into Banff and Lake Louise. It was the travel centre, the commercial centre, the food distribution centre, the postal centre and the communications centre, where you could communicate with the world by telegram or telephone. The station was a distinct community, complete with the most popular coffee shop and the best gossip in town.

The express office was already humming in early morning, sorting the town deliveries that had arrived on Train 1 at 1:30 a.m. Percy Reeves would be loading the delivery truck for residential and commercial deliveries. In the summer, Percy had a helper, usually a student, for the town deliveries. John Stuckert (my pal Johnnie's dad) was the warehouseman, and he'd be busy stacking the outgoing express on the carts for loading on Train 2 at 9:55 a.m. or the Dominions in late morning. He'd also help unload the reefer cars that had been shunted onto the west end Willow Tracks. In peak season, up to half a dozen reefer cars arrived daily.

By 9:00 a.m., the activity level around the station was intense.

Hotel transfer buses, limos and private cars arrived at the west end of the station, disgorging their passengers for the eastbound Train 2 or the westbound Dominions an hour later. The Cascade, King Edward and Mount Royal hotels had their own buses, and the Homestead transfer vehicle was a meticulously restored 1936 Packard limousine. A couple of taxis would arrive, one from Legion Taxi, with Rocky Beatty at the wheel, or George McKenzie, owner of Cascade Taxi. Charlie Harbidge would arrive in the mail truck with large canvas bags full of mail from the downtown post office and the Banff Springs Hotel. The newsstand would be packed with the bus drivers, taxi operators and locals who habituated the station for a mug of Bill Young's excellent CPR coffee and his even better stories. It was all very social, with tidbits of gossip, good-natured joshing and a few laughs.

After checking their luggage in the baggage room, outbound passengers would gather at the newsstand, drinking coffee or purchasing souvenirs from Cora, Bill's wife, who was the keeper of the cash. Their employee, Frances Horinek, a young lady who came for a couple of summers and ended up staying over 20 years, would be scurrying around, refilling coffee mugs and stocking up the sandwich trays, cookie jars and pastry flats in preparation for the arriving train. Bill's dog Paddy, a highly pedigreed Chesapeake Bay Retriever, occupied the first seat on the bench nearest the newsstand, entertaining passengers with a bag of tricks Bill had taught him over the years. Photographed by tourists from around the world, Paddy was once the subject of a feature story by Nicholas Morant in Canadian Pacific's *Spanner Magazine*, so his fame spread far beyond Banff.

Every summer in the early 1950s, Dougie Young, Bill and Cora's nephew, visited for a few weeks. Most days, Doug and I took Paddy for a walk, but with strict orders not to allow him off the leash, reasoning that if Paddy ran loose, it would be detrimental to his show dog training. I suspect he was worried that the dog might take off and we'd never find him. One time we disregarded the warning and turned Paddy loose. He was off like a shot, chasing the squirrels, splashing and swimming in the creek and doing what dogs love best, rolling in fresh manure. We returned to the station with horse manure matted in his wiry fur and an overpowering smell. Bill knew instantly we had let Paddy loose and never asked us to walk the dog again.

In the ticket office, Ed Shaw would be busy confirming reservations and processing tickets for departing passengers. Dad, as station agent, would be checking invoices, preparing the bank deposits, completing the daily balance sheets and scheduling the freight deliveries to the merchants. Directly behind Dad's desk was the operator's desk and nerve centre of the station. The operator would be busy preparing the train orders for the engineer and the conductor of the next incoming train, having earlier received traffic instructions from central dispatch in Calgary. The orders were written on one or more "flimsies," the messages coded in numbers, instructing the engineer where the next "meet" would occur and which train would take the siding. The orders were secured in the spring mechanism of the "hoop," which had a six-foot handle. As the train thundered into the station, the operator would stand on the edge of the platform, holding the hoop straight up, and the engineer, leaning out of the cab, would snag the hoop with his right arm, removing the train orders. The hoop was thrown clear and retrieved by the operator. Obviously, an engineer had to be well schooled in deciphering the train orders, but he had to be a better hoop catcher.

As Train 2 eased into the depot, Station Master Bob Fulton

would make his arrival announcement, requesting passengers to stand back from the edge of the platform and wait until detraining passengers were clear before boarding. Many through passengers would detrain and scamper to the newsstand for coffee, sandwiches or snacks. The arriving passengers were guided to the kiosk at the west end of the station to board a hotel bus or hail a taxi. Mister Everything, George Murray, manned the information kiosk for Brewster. He booked accommodation for anyone without reservations and sold sightseeing, pack trips and canoe rentals, always lending a sympathetic ear to those requiring extra assistance. For over 30 years, George was the problem solver and greeter par excellence; any company would have been proud to employ him. For many, he was the first contact in Banff and sent them happily on their way to enjoy their vacation. George also mentored many of the young folks employed for the summer and away from home.

While the platform was buzzing with activity, the baggage porters were at the head end baggage car, scrambling to load and unload the luggage. Arrivals and departures were a slick operation, efficient and entirely manual. A baggage porter became fit after a summer season.

Ten minutes later, Bob Fulton would make his boarding announcement: "All aboooooard for Train 2, departing for Canmore, Exshaw, Cochrane, Calgary, Medicine Hat, Moose Jaw, Regina, Brandon, Winnipeg, Dryden, Port Arthur, Fort William, Sudbury, Toronto, Ottawa and Montreal. All aboooooard, this is your final call." Ensuring all stepping stools and vestibule doors were closed, he'd give the highball to the engineer and, just like that, the train was gone. Bob's reciting almost every stop between Banff and Toronto equalled a lesson in Canadian geography.

No sooner had Train 2 left the station when the westbound Mountaineer arrived at 10:15 a.m. Waiting in "the hole" (a side track east of the station), the Mountaineer returned to the main line and steamed into the depot. Again, Station Master Fulton made the arrival announcement and once again the platform activity began. The Mountaineer had a slightly longer stop in Banff due to the switching and servicing requirements. On most arrivals, sleeping or dining car equipment was added or deleted while the service crew iced the cars not only for refrigeration but as the coolant for the air conditioning.

Arriving tour groups would board awaiting buses for a day of sightseeing before hotel check-in, so the luggage was sent ahead to the hotels. The sleeping cars (and coach cars for the budget operators) were switched off the Mountaineer onto the parking tracks located at the east end of the station. The four parallel tracks became officially know as the Garden Tracks as they abutted up to the sprawling rock garden decorating the station grounds. Another set of parking tracks, located at the west end of the station, was called the Willow Tracks because about 220 yards of golden willows had been planted along these tracks in 1939, commemorating the royal visit. The two Willow Tracks had a dual purpose by providing shade for the elegant private railcars of Canadian Pacific executives (president, regional superintendents and other high-level dignitaries) visiting Banff. Inlaid teak and mahogany panelling decorated their bedroom, lounge and dining areas, and private chefs oversaw their kitchens. The other purpose of the Willow Tracks was much more functional: refrigerated express cars would be shunted to the Willow Tracks, convenient to the adjacent express office, for unloading.

After the Banff stopover, the groups would reboard the

railcars a day or two later and continue the journey to Vancouver. Due to the limited hotel space, some tour groups stayed on the Pullman sleeping cars during their Banff stopover and an accompanying dining car provided breakfast and dinner.

After the designated arrivals were switched onto the Garden Tracks, any departing sleepers were added to the Mountaineer. These sleepers (or coaches) had arrived a day or two earlier and the assigned tour had completed the Banff stopover. But the occupants did not board the Mountaineer in Banff. Instead, they toured by motorcoach to Moraine Lake, Lake Louise and then through the Kicking Horse Pass to Field, BC, where they would reboard the train.

The luggage for departing groups arrived at the station by 9:00 a.m., in special baggage-only buses. Loaded onto platform carts and pulled to the Garden Tracks, the redcaps would space the bags in the designated sleeping compartments. The system was manual, but it worked, and few bags were ever misplaced. The bus drivers passed along the bag count to the redcaps, the tour escorts would confirm that count and redcaps would then load and space the bags. The counts had to match, to ensure all bags were on board.

Adding or deleting sleeping cars and coaches in Banff was characteristic of the Mountaineer since Banff was a two- or three-night stay and *the* major attraction in most Canadian Rockies travel brochures. The sleeping car porters stayed on board during stopovers, refreshing the compartments with new towels, pillowslips and linens. The dining cars would take on uniforms, tablecloths and kitchen linens, while napkins and soiled linens were placed in large canvas bags stacked on the platform. The baggage porters collected the bags and sent them on the baggage car to the regional laundry in Calgary. After fermenting in the sun for a day, the dirty linen aroma was putrid. During the trip to Calgary, the baggage car attendants would often leave the doors wide open.

Most of the sleeping cars that overnighted on the Garden Tracks at the east end of the station were olive green cars, leased from the Pullman Car Company of Chicago. A leased sleeping car included the porter, and the diners came with a full contingent of kitchen and wait staff. Most Pullmans were mechanically air-conditioned but required steam for heating. Until 1952, the switch engine used to hook up to these cars at night to provide the steam heat, but, in 1952, due to increasing volume, an oil-fired steam plant was built for the Garden Tracks just below the east end of the rock garden. The Garden Tracks could easily accommodate up to 25 cars and all could be connected to steam heat. Power boxes were located along each track for lighting, as well as recharging the heavy-duty batteries powering the air conditioning. Adjacent to the Garden Tracks were men's and lady's washrooms, all equipped with showers for the sleeping-car occupants.

After the departure of the Mountaineer, there was little time to relax as the hotel buses were back again with passengers for the westbound Dominions. The Toronto Dominion arrived at 11:30 a.m., and another round of feverish loading and unloading was underway. The train was barely out of the station when the Montreal Dominion arrived at 12:05 p.m. Since the Dominions were Canadian Pacific's crack transcontinental trains (until 1955), their arrivals and departures were the busiest of the day.

Over the summer months, extra CP sleepers and dining cars were often added in Banff to the westbound Dominions. For these additions, the switching crew had to be on the ball as the station stop for the Dominion was only ten minutes. As soon as the train arrived, the switch crew would cut the tail end car from the train, connect it to the sleepers spotted on the adjacent track and recouple to the train. Adding the additional equipment to the tail end allowed uninterrupted boarding for the rest of the train. When the switching manoeuvre was complete, the station master would make the departure announcement and give the engineer the highball to depart.

A welcome lull followed the Dominion's departure but was short-lived as luggage began to arrive for the eastbound Mountaineer. Although the train didn't arrive until 4:15 p.m., the baggage buses from the downtown hotels and the Chateau Lake Louise began to unload around 2:00 p.m. The redcaps went flat out, spacing the carry-on luggage onto the Pullmans parked on the Garden Tracks. Around 3:30 p.m., the tour groups began to arrive, preboarding their Pullmans. Around 4:15 p.m., the switch engine and crew would pull the Pullman cars out of the Garden Tracks, "spotting" (positioning) them next to the main line. The eastbound Mountaineer arrived at 4:35 p.m., and as soon as the arriving passengers had disembarked the train would be split in two, with the Pullmans inserted into the middle of the consist. Once the train was joined again, final boarding commenced, and the Mountaineer would depart for the two-day journey to Minneapolis and St. Paul and Chicago.

The next wave of departing passengers arrived from the hotels to depart on the eastbound Dominions. The Montreal Dominion arrived at 5:15 p.m., bringing another flurry of activity, and departed at 5:25 p.m. The Toronto Dominion arrived 30 minutes later at 5:55 p.m. The eastbound Dominions required little switching activity. If any sleeping cars were vacant after Banff, they would travel through to Calgary, a major divisional point and maintenance centre.

The newsstand, ticket office and baggage room were closed after the departure of the Dominion, but, during the summer, the telegraph and telephone office remained open until midnight, fielding calls from guests at the Chateau Lake Louise and Banff Springs requiring long-distance assistance. Canadian Pacific had all those bases covered too.

You could sense the collective sigh of relief after the Dominion's departure, marking the end of the day. All was quiet until 1:30 a.m., when Train 1, the all-stops westbound, arrived and the circus began again.

EXPRESS AND FREIGHT: THE COMMUNITY LIFEBLOOD

Supporting a community of 2,000 residents, and a summer population that swelled to over 10,000, was no easy feat considering the trains were the aggregate suppliers of all the town's needs, including the tourists. But the express and freight offices carried the ball.

CP Express handled all incoming shipments of dry goods and foodstuffs for the grocery stores, butcher shops, hotels, resorts and restaurants. It was the FedEx and UPS of the day for the merchandisers who required expedited delivery of small packages, appliances, souvenirs or car parts. In addition, a daily summer schedule delivered to Lake Louise, Johnston's Canyon and Mount Eisenhower Bungalows. CP Hotels ran their own supply trucks in the summer, loading from the refrigerated reefer cars parked adjacent to the station on the Willow Tracks.

Bill Hoffman was the express department manager during my years at the station, and the huge volume of goods managed daily by Bill's crew seemed an impossible task. On most summer days, Bill's crew would unload and deliver up to seven boxcars of foodstuffs alone, plus regular express arriving on trains throughout the day. John Stuckert Sr., the warehouse foreman, emptied and filled the warehouse at least a couple of times every day, sorting the deliveries for the trucks and working the counter servicing those who picked up or dropped off consignments. Mr. Stuckert had been an aspiring baseball player in the 1930s with the Granum Red Sox in the Prairie Baseball League and selflessly shared his talent with kids who wanted to play organized ball. He coached both little league and pony league teams throughout my school years.

No one, not even the young kids brought in for summer help, could keep up to Percy Reeves, the senior driver, who by that time was in his late 50s. Percy had his own routines for every task and, after years of heavy lifting, had it down to a science. Percy was like the Energizer bunny – he just kept going and going.

The freight office was in the train station and the storage shed was directly across the tracks. Freight, to differentiate from express, included heavy-duty merchandise, bulk products, building supplies, automobiles and any nature of nonperishable supplies that did not require expedited delivery. Long distance, or "through freights," from eastern Canada or Vancouver would "set off" (drop) freight cars in Calgary with goods for local destinations like Banff. The freight cars would be mustered together to make up a local train or "way freight," delivering the goods to the respective towns. The Banff way freight was a mix of freight cars carrying heavy merchandise, tanker cars from Alberta refineries for the local bulk stations and flat cars or gondola cars loaded with cement or lumber for local contractors and Unwin's Lumberyard.

There were at least two services a week to Banff, depending on the season. On its arrival in Banff, the train engineer, in conjunction with Dusty and his switch crew, would position the tanker cars on the track by the pumping station, where they would be unhitched, separated from the train and the contents pumped to fill the respective storage tanks for Texaco, Esso or British American (BA). Each entity had its own fleet of trucks, delivering to the various company and independent service stations. In the early '50s, Banff had two Esso stations, two BA, two Texaco, one White Rose and one North Star station. Two more Esso stations were located at Lake Louise and Johnston's Canyon, and Eisenhower Bungalows operated service stations in the summer months. Brewster Transport operated service stations at Field and the Columbia Icefield, and George Brewster had a service station at Saskatchewan River Crossing. Additionally, the bulk dealers had federal government contracts, plus lucrative contracts were up for grabs when construction began on the Trans-Canada Highway through the park in 1953. The bulk plants at the station were busy operations, especially during the summer months.

The Banff-destined freight cars would be set off on the siding track (#5) in front of the freight shed. Some boxcar shipments would be directly off-loaded into the freight shed, but the shipments including machinery, heavy equipment and automobiles would remain in the boxcars until the vendor arrived to claim the goods. A sturdy wooden ramp was trackside in front of the freight shed doors, allowing trucks to access the loading dock. Charlie Harbidge, a local cartage operator, delivered most of the freight to the businesses. The flat cars, loaded with timber and building supplies, were set off next to the ice house adjacent to Unwin's warehouse.

As station agent, my dad was also the freight agent, overseeing all freight, tanker and lumber activity. Occasionally, he'd take me with him to the freight shed when releasing a consignment of goods he thought would be fun for me to see, especially the luxury cars of the day.

The automobile boxcars had extra-wide doors, expediting loading and unloading. Steel runners were positioned from the platform into the boxcar. As the platform was the same height as the boxcar doors, you simply drove the automobile onto the platform and down to the service road. Dad would sometimes allow me to sit in the front seat of one of the fancy cars as he manoeuvred it out of the boxcar; that was a real treat for me.

After the way freight departed, and the boxcars unloaded, the freight shed would be jammed with all imaginable merchandise. Banff was a growing community recovering from the material shortages and rationing of the Second World War. Machinery, tools, building supplies, stoves and furniture were no longer unattainable luxuries, and refrigerators were the flavour of the month, fast replacing iceboxes. It was somewhat ironic that Charlie Harbidge, owner of a local cartage company, would be delivering the refrigerators that would eventually end his home delivery ice business. Television took its time to come to the Bow Valley, but the Adams Electric truck would be seen almost daily, loading fridges, stoves, washing machines and the latest thing called a clothes dryer. In 1954, Adams Electric led the charge to place a repeater station on Mount Norquay to deflect the television waves into the valley. That made for mighty fine reception of a snowy test pattern during the day and hazy images during the broadcast hours, starting at five o'clock with the children's program, ending with the CBC news at 11:00 p.m. CKRD-TV, Red Deer, was Banff's first TV station. For whatever reason, the TV signal from Red Deer was much stronger than the signal from Calgary.

THE STATION ORCHESTRA: CONDUCTORS, PHOTOGRAPHERS AND CONCESSIONAIRES

Any day at the station played out like a symphony on the rails. Arriving trains were separated and switched to sidings. The cars were serviced, the consists reassembled and, miraculously, in a matter of minutes, the trains were back at the platform ready to board. It was a performance worth witnessing: a huge locomotive shunted the railcars around the yard, then gently eased to a crawl, coupling cars together, as the switch crew jumped in between, connecting the steam and air hoses. To the uninitiated, the switching movements might have been terrifying to watch, but there was a certain grace in the crew's movements as they laboured under tons of steel, inches from the wheels of the locomotive.

Dusty Miller was not only the switch crew conductor but also the social convener for the summer crews. Like Dusty, most of the switch crew had families in Calgary and accepted the Banff postings because of overtime and the away-from-home bonuses. Dusty took it on himself to ensure the boys had a good time. One summer, he built a brick and mortar barbeque next to the bunkhouse and his cookouts were as famous as his card games. But his true talent was orchestrating the show as his crew played the trains like toys on a set.

Every evening Dusty received the game plan for the following day from Bob Fulton, the station master, and Tom Egan, the sleeping and dining car manager. Most of the switching movements involved the Mountaineers, but often equipment changes were required on the Dominions as well. Every afternoon, with information from the chief dispatcher in Calgary, Fulton would compile all passenger train movements for the following day, including car names, numbers and complete consists. Fulton would collaborate with Egan, who had received similar information on the status of the sleeping and dining cars arriving in Banff: what cars to be set aside or added to meet booking requirements.

The Passenger and Sleeping Car Reservations Department for western Canada was headquartered in Winnipeg, Manitoba, and confirmed all passenger and sleeping car reservations across the west. This office distributed the confirmed reservation requirements to central dispatch, which then built the equipment requirements of future departures. Extra sleeping cars were assigned to the Banff yard as needed, and a summer office was opened to specifically oversee these requirements.

Tom Egan, usually based in Winnipeg, was assigned to Banff in the summer months. His position was unique; in addition to regular duties, he was required to maintain a high-profile public relations function at the Banff Springs Hotel, mingling with the dignitaries, the Hollywood stars and the monied, who came to Banff for extended stays and booked first-class accommodation on the trains. Tall, slim and stylish, he had all the attributes of a polished PR professional, and his personality, sense of humour and love of life endeared him to all. He was a lesson in communication and an early role model for me. I always imagined that a job like his would be the ultimate position with the railway.

Bob Fulton had the total opposite demeanour: he was a listener and reserved, but you could sense the strength of his character when he spoke. He was obsessively organized and efficient, and a perfect fit for his job. The daily train movements were like a jigsaw puzzle and Bob, like his title, was the master of the game. He provided Dusty, his conductor, with flawless plans for the day's activities.

If the station orchestra had a choreographer, it might have been Nicholas Morant. Morant was famous in North America for his stunning railway photography, and his name is forever linked with the Canadian Pacific Railway. From 1935 through 1981, as special photographer, CPR, he was constantly on assignment from coast to coast, photographing the entire CPR portfolio, including passenger and freight train services, CP Hotels and often travel abroad with Canadian Pacific Steamships or Canadian Pacific Airlines. He photographed people, places and historic occurrences, as well as other CP portfolios, including Marathon Realty and CP Oil & Gas.

I met Mr. Morant sometime after we moved to Banff, but during my working years at the station I got to know him as Nick. Throughout the summer months, we'd load and unload his photo equipment onto the baggage car when he departed or returned from his photo shoots. His equipment, including cameras, reflectors, scaffolding and other paraphernalia, was stored in a corner of the baggage room. Nick was a mesmerizing storyteller; his harrowing account of a grizzly attack in Yoho National Park stayed foremost in my mind when hiking in the mountains. Many of his Banff promotional photo shoots captured scenes during train arrivals, with the switch crew in action.

The group tour business that poured into the Banff Springs Hotel every summer also brought another talented photographer and unforgettable character to Banff. In the summer of

1954, Johnny Owen and his wife Muriel assumed the photo concession at the Banff Springs, beginning their long-time residency. I met John at the station when I began working in the baggage room. During the summer season, John was at the station daily, taking the group photos for the various tour groups departing on the Mountaineer. On occasion, he'd capture individual shots of guests boarding the train. A favourite shot was to have Dusty position the locomotive along the platform and the guests would appear to climb the steps up to the cab.

John's favourite location for group photos at the station was the rock garden at the east end of the station, where visitors often awaited train arrivals and departures. A Rundle stone pathway and stairs led to the secluded meditation garden, set in a copse of trees on top of the sandhill behind the station. Vic Sugg, CP's first gardener in Banff, had created the beautiful setting. Vic had also designed and built the flowered traffic control circle in front of the station as part of the company's cross-country initiative to beautify station properties in 1923.

Concessionaires at the Banff Springs, the Owens were required to provide their own housing. In 1956, they decided on permanent roots in Banff and purchased a quaint log cabin on Glen Avenue. They expanded the cabin into a fabulous log home, moving another log structure from Golden to Banff. The two were artfully joined together, and this classic log home is one of the finest residences in the town of Banff.

John and Muriel were famous for their hospitality, hosting cocktail parties and BBQs for friends and special guests of the Banff Springs Hotel. When the Owens established their specialty tour company for photographers, their location on the Bow River provided the perfect atmosphere for the wind-up dinners. John's story about his pal, and fellow station orchestra member, Tom Egan, was a classic. One night, after a cocktail party, Tom had announced he was heading for home, but it was obvious he might have some trouble piloting his car. As John said, "The driveway was little more than a track through the trees, so I offered to back his car out to the road." Tom said, "Nope, I'll be fine, I know where the trees are." John went back into the house only to hear a crunch seconds later. "I ran back outside and there was Egan, with a sheepish grin on his face. 'See John? I told you I know where the trees are – I got one!'"

During the lead-up to Christmas, the Owens dressed as Mr. and Mrs. Claus, driving a horse-drawn sleigh around to Banff homes delivering Christmas cheer. As their children, Cindy and Gordy, grew, they'd dress as Santa's elves, accompanying their parents. When the Banff Springs Hotel opened on a year-round basis, they would arrive at the Mount Steven Hall amid strains of "Here Comes Santa Claus." The family was synonymous with Christmas Eve, and many a child who questioned the Santa Claus story had their faith extended by a couple of years after their encounter with Mr. and Mrs. Claus.

Reminiscing about the old days and the newsstand as the primo meeting place in Banff recently, I was asked about what locals frequented it. I replied, "A better question to ask is who didn't habituate the station? It's a shorter list."

THE BAGGAGE ROOM

The spring of 1957 marked what I considered my return to life at the Banff station, even if I no longer lived there. Finally, I was 15, old enough to work for the CPR, and I immediately applied for a baggage room position. Merle recommended me, and Walter Richmond, who had replaced my dad as station agent in 1955, approved my application. I was in seventh heaven. I was back!

I started work on weekends in mid-May until school was out in June. All winter I was impatient to start, but as the day approached, I became increasingly apprehensive. It was the first time I would work entirely with adults and career railroaders. The job demanded punctuality, attention to detail and some heavy lifting, all a little alien to a teenager. Brother Fred, sensing my insecurity, had loads of fun razzing me that I was too small to handle the heavy luggage, or wouldn't be able to get up in the mornings. Unlike today's world of automated baggage handling, our tasks were manual and there was little tolerance for mistakes. When my training began, Merle oversaw the indoctrination and initially I was overwhelmed. There were forms for everything, to be filled out in triplicate and filed daily. Cash reports had to be prepared, and daily reports listing all unclaimed luggage submitted. But after a couple of weekends, it began to make sense and the system worked. In my seven years at the station, I do not recall a lost bag.

With a pecking order in place, and as the junior employee, I had some hazing to endure. Ostensibly, it was in good fun, but the underlying message was loud and clear: you're entering the adult world. I soon learned you did what you were told. My first shift began 30 minutes prior to the arrival of the other staff, and on arrival I was presented with a large push broom and instructed to sweep the entire baggage warehouse. The flooring was rough planks and the warehouse area about 3,000 square feet. It was a long, dusty, sweaty hour of sweeping, and I thought I'd choke to death. Merle chuckled after I finished and said, "By the way, next time scatter some Endust on the floor. It keeps the dust down." After this initiation, sweeping the warehouse floor remained part of my job, but I always had a helper and, of course, some Endust (a green, chemically treated powder).

The baggage room opened at 8:00 a.m., an hour prior to the arrival of the first train, to accept checked luggage. The train ticket was required to verify the routing and destination. If travelling exclusively on CP trains, only the final destination was required to be stamped on the luggage tag, secured to the handle by strong twine. The passenger was issued a matching claim check required to claim luggage at the destination. All luggage check numbers and destinations were listed on a manifest; one copy for the attendant on the baggage car, one for the baggage room and a copy submitted daily to central dispatch.

However, if the destination was in the United States, a multipart "interline" claim check was issued. The routing and name of every railroad was listed on the baggage check as per the client's ticket. A typical routing might be "CP to Portal, Soo to St. Paul, C & NW to Chicago and NYC to New York." The double and triple documentation for checked luggage sometimes seemed like overkill, until a bag trace was required. Then it was golden.

Prior to train arrival, we'd pull the loaded carts down the

platform to the baggage car, along with a couple of empty carts. The Banff-destined luggage, stacked and waiting in the doorway, was off-loaded, and then the departing luggage placed on board. The procedure had to be quick; with one exception of the Mountaineer, Banff was but a ten-minute stop. A delayed departure was not an option, because it risked the wrath of the station master standing on the platform, with his classic railway watch in hand, counting down the seconds to his *all abooooooard* announcement.

Our manual procedures were efficient, but train times remained a mad scramble. On an average day, 800 to 1,000 passengers would pass through the station. In the late 1950s, morning trains were back to back; the westbound Mountaineer arrived at 9:10 a.m., often followed by a second section within minutes, and the Dominion arrived at 10:10. In the afternoon, activity would begin to build about 1:30 p.m., in preparation for the westbound Canadian at 2:45 p.m. and the eastbound Canadian 40 minutes later. At 4:00 p.m., the eastbound Mountaineer arrived, the passengers disembarked and the Banff luggage unloaded. The consist was then moved to a parking track and switching operations began. By 5:15, the Mountaineer was back at the platform for final boarding, and we'd load the checked luggage for the 5:30 departure. At 6:15 p.m., the eastbound Dominion rolled into the station, usually the busiest arrival of the day. Arriving luggage was often three or four carts stacked high. It was no treat pulling the carts back to the station, and some days, if the engineer miscalculated his stop, the baggage car ended up off the platform. The long haul back to the station was a back-breaker and we knew the detraining passengers would be impatient to claim their belongings.

The departure of the Dominion was a welcome end to the day.

Closing procedures included the bundling of the day's records and submitting the cash remittance to the ticket office. The floors were swept, the garbage taken out and all doors locked. Everything was ready to go for another day.

LUNCHTIME FISHING AND THE QUARTERS GAME: STRANGE PERKS?

In the spring of 1958, instead of guiding fishermen like he had been the previous two summers, Jim Alexander began work in the baggage room with me. But Jim never left his love of fishing behind, and most evenings and sometimes during lunch hour we'd race off together to one of our fishing holes. Acquaintances who didn't work at the station expressed outright disbelief at our lunchtime fishing adventures.

Our regular workday at the station was based on an eight-hour shift spread over 11 hours, from eight in the morning to seven at night, but we seldom finished before 7:30 or 8:00. Overtime was nonexistent. If a train was late, you stayed late, and it was your responsibility to figure out the difference later. Therefore, a two-hour lunch was entirely possible, as long as someone was around between noon and 2:00 p.m. to check incoming luggage.

Jim and I were still in high school, enjoying the fruits of summer life. Our baggage room partner was a student from Prince Edward Island (immediately christened "Spud"). Spud was older, and his mission was to save money and finish university. He covered for us when we were a little tardy returning from our lunch-hour expeditions. In return, we'd cover the evening Dominion and Spud could leave at 5:30, after the departure of the Mountaineer.

Our favourite spot was on the Bow River, near the bottom

of the golf course loop road, about a 15-minute drive from the train station. We'd access the river through the elk fence and wade across a swift channel to the island. This was possible only in early spring or after the runoff subsided in midsummer. A short hike through dense bush took you across the island, and there, on a 90-degree river bend, a huge logjam had been created by years of high water. Though the best trout fishing anywhere on the Bow, it was a tough place to catch them.

When a fish did hit your lure, you had to lead it into the swift current, clearing the brush and submerged logs. If you slipped, you could drop a leg through a hole in the logjam or, worse, end up in the current. But with Jim's savvy and lots of practice, we often caught two- and three-pound rainbows or brown trout. On one occasion, Jim hooked and landed a huge six-pounder. In a heavy current, this was like hooking a ten-pound fish and the fight every fisherman dreams about.

One lunchtime, Jim and I went off to catch a mess of fish for a BBQ that evening. We fished the logjam, caught a couple of beauties and looped a line through their gills to keep them fresh, securing the line to a large spike driven into the riverbank. Off we went to another bend in the river and hooked a couple more. With enough fish to feed everyone, we headed back to retrieve our previous catch. The fish were gone! Had the fish somehow loosened the spike and swam away? But, on closer inspection, we saw a skid mark through the mud and in the tall grass along the riverbank, the spike and the remains of one fish. A marten had outsmarted us! We went back to work with a fish story that no one believed (and dinner was tube steaks).

We seldom struck out when we fished Forty Mile or Whiskey creeks, and both were handy to the station. We'd have our lines in the water within minutes. In late August and early September, the fishing was exceptional; the bull trout were beginning their spawning run and it was almost too easy to catch your limit. Bull trout are voracious feeders and they would have a go at almost any bait or lure.

But it wasn't always fishing during downtimes. Waiting in between trains or for late arrivals created other distractions and strange perks that were always a mixture of fun and games. Our greatest distraction was "pitching quarters." The baggage room boys, the redcaps, the Pullman crew and various bus drivers would gather in the extra-wide doorway of the baggage room and the game was on.

At the edge of the platform, 8 x 8 solid fir beams about 12 feet long had been installed as bumpers to stop vehicles from backing up too far when unloading, and to protect the overhanging roof. From a line on the floor just inside the baggage room door, the distance to the beam was a measured ten feet. It was a basic game: you stood on the line and pitched your quarter toward the beam. Whoever tossed their quarter closest to the beam was the winner. But if your quarter rolled and leaned against the beam, the "leaner" was the winner and all participants had to pay double. The only way to beat a "leaner" was to throw a "topper," bouncing your quarter off the pavement and landing it on top of the beam. If you landed a topper, everyone paid triple. Every minute there was a new champ.

Most days, at least half a dozen fortune seekers participated. It wasn't difficult to win or lose ten dollars in an hour. Considering the average rate of pay was about 12 dollars a day, a novice to the game could easily lose a day's wages before the first train rolled into the station.

Jim and I were the consistent winners. There was no mystery to our skills; we practised and played every single day and either one of us could land a "topper" every third or fourth toss. But, like all games of chance, the participants were convinced they'd win and we were happy to encourage them. Our daily take could be as much as 15 to 20 dollars. In the '50s, that was a lot of "mad money."

REDCAP DAYS: THE TOP OF MY WORLD

Long before I was old enough to work, it had been my goal to be a redcap. In the spring of 1959, a position opened up and Mr. Newell, the recently appointed station agent, accepted my application. I had finally made it to the top of my world!

My brother Fred and Wayne Ferguson, both long-term redcaps, had moved on, but I would join my classmate and pal Johnny Stuckert. I had always wanted to work with my big brother, but after six summers he was ready for a change and had joined Parks Canada at the campground as an attendant and interpreter, conducting evening presentations around the campfire for the park visitors.

Fred's first summer as a redcap had been in 1953, so he was already a seasoned veteran by the time I began working in the baggage room. He was best remembered as the groundbreaker for the redcaps, as he was instrumental in making the position as lucrative as it became.

In year two, Fred assumed the position of head redcap and, as such, had close relationships with the escorts of the numerous tour groups coming to Banff. That was the benchmark summer when he instituted the tipping guidelines for tour companies, benefitting all redcaps that were to follow in his footsteps. In his words,

> The job was 7 days a week with no days off or set hours; we simply had to meet all passenger trains. If the

trains were late, then we worked late. One day a mudslide near Field, BC, delayed the trains coming from the west, and the first one did not arrive in Banff until midnight. It was probably during this wait for the trains that I met my mentor. Happiness Tours was one of the larger tour companies of the day and had so many departures throughout the summer that they posted a tour manager in Banff to ensure all arrangements went smoothly, as well as providing an on-site resource for the tour escorts. His name was G.A. (Curly) Reeves and we became good friends. Curly had been around the block and had all the angles covered, with valuable insider advice on how to deal with the tour escorts. As the redcap job only paid $160.00 per month, tips from the tours were a potential gold mine. When Curly asked me how much the Banff redcaps charged per bag, I had to tell him that the CPR would not let us mandate a per bag charge, simply relying on the generosity of the tour escort. He replied that all American redcaps charge per bag and therefore would pay us the same per bag that they pay in the USA. From that day we charged 20 cents per bag. One tour group had 500 bags and paid us $100. That was a lot of money in the 1950s. This went on all summer and the other tour escorts fell into line. The precedent had been set and thanks to Curly, it put me through university.

Curly was a mathematics professor at the University of Florida but had worked summers in various capacities for Happiness Tours since he was a student. Curly often visited in the baggage room and one evening heard Fred strumming his ukulele, singing with his co-workers. Fred's wooden ukulele, carted around to parties and wiener roasts over the years, had seen better days. Curly would often join in, and when he returned the following summer, he gifted Fred with a banjo ukulele he had bought in his university days. Years later, Fred took the banjo uke for repairs and a tune up only to find he was the owner of a rare and valuable instrument, which he still plays.

Curly's stories of the travel business were mesmerizing and he'd been everywhere, escorting tours to places I didn't even know existed. One day I asked Curly why people would travel with his company to Banff when anyone could buy a train ticket and hotel room? Professor Curly gave me the quick version of Tourism 101, explaining how tour companies operated and prospered, how the concept of bulk rates and volume buying strengthened negotiations with vendors. The operator would conglomerate all package inclusions and then break them down to per-person rates, based on the number of passengers travelling. To this sum, a markup was added, providing the profit margin, from which sales commissions were paid.

Curly went on to explain how tour companies would use the huge sums of money received in deposits and prepayments to play the foreign exchange market or simply place the funds in short-term deposits, earning over 10 per cent interest from banks. Most operators were on credit with vendors, paying on receipt of invoice at least 30 days (and sometimes 60) after travel was completed, meaning they could play with customer deposits and prepayments for months. When payment was made to the vendors, foreign exchange and interest profits were often more than the profit margin of the tour packages. It boggled my mind, but I went away with a new understanding of the industry. Little did I know then how valuable that knowledge would be later in my life.

I had similar discussions with other escorts, most of whom were eager to tell a hick from Banff how much they knew. By showing undivided interest, eventually I'd get the whole story. The summer of 1959 flew by for me. I was working in paradise, meeting people from all walks of life, fuelling my hunger to explore. I loved working the sleeping cars, spacing the luggage and imagining my own great train journey. Over the season, I memorized the floor plans of every sleeping car: the Glen cars with all roomettes; the heavyweight sleepers with sections, compartments and a drawing room; the tourist-class sleepers with sections only; and the configurations of the sleek new stainless steel streamliner cars of the Canadian, including the Manor, Chateau and Park cars. Best of all, the hard physical work of slinging a few hundred bags every day made me feel alive. This skinny runt was finally bulking up.

The summer of 1959 was also a social bonanza for me; I met a whole kaleidoscope of new friends. In late spring, I was hanging out on Banff Avenue in front of Andrianne's Restaurant with Jim and schoolmate Bill McKenzie, awaiting the crowd to empty out from the Lux Theatre. Bill had just started his summer job as a lifeguard at the Cave and Basin swimming pool and, in the crush of folks coming down the street, pointed out a tall skinny guy, with horn-rimmed glasses and a brush cut, saying, "Get a load of this guy. He's one of the new lifeguards this year; we've got a couple of dandies." At almost the same time, a 1954, two-tone blue and white Pontiac convertible pulled over and bounced up onto the curb. The driver, with a slightly chubby baby face and blond hair, called out to Bill in a squeaky voice: "Hey pal, what happens in Banff on a Sunday night?" Bill turned to me and said, "That's the other one."

Our lives were never to be the same. We had just met Tom

Shields and Wayne King and the chemistry was instant; we were from completely different backgrounds but seemed to share something. That summer I felt my attitudes starting to shift as my world expanded, as if I had new eyes and ears. This wasn't high school anymore and Jim and I were willing subjects for change.

In the weeks that followed, we met Tom and Wayne's pals. They were all a couple of years older than us, but that didn't seem to matter anymore. Chuck Cook, Clark Rimmer and Grant Styles became instant pals, and this was the beginning of "The Boys and Girls from Banff," as we call our gang to this day.

Coming from different backgrounds would be an understatement: Jim and I were mountain boys from small town Banff and close-knit families. Tom was from Grand Prairie, Alberta, and had lost his dad. Wayne was from Kitchener, Ontario, and had lost both of his parents at 12. After bouncing around between older brothers and sisters, he made the split and headed west at the wise old age of 14. Chuck was from Stettler, Alberta, and his dad was in the oil patch (of which I'd never heard), and Clark was a dryland farm boy from Foremost, Alberta. Grant was a world apart too, a city guy from Mount Royal in Calgary, but he fell in with our mob soon after arriving in Banff. There was no logical reason why we all bonded, but Banff was the catalyst and we became family.

We did have one thing in common. In the late '50s and early '60s, there was no texting and none of us had phones. Nevertheless, we always managed to communicate daily, meeting somewhere after work to plan our evening. The meeting place soon became the train station, where there was plenty of action, and this mob, like many other folks in Banff, came to watch the people and the trains. The station community captured everyone.

The year 1959 was not a landmark one for tourism, but I had no previous experience as a redcap to make comparisons. All I knew was that I'd never made so much money before, most of it in tips. But with the apparent drop in ridership that summer, the rumours began that CPR was considering the cancellation of the Mountaineer, amalgamating it with the Dominion and joining the two trains together at Moose Jaw, Saskatchewan. While I knew I'd be returning to my job the following summer, I was concerned about the impact the changes might have on my summer income. But, fortunately, the hype had begun for the 1962 Seattle World's Fair and CP decided to maintain the status quo, expecting the Mountaineer to have a bounce-back year in 1960.

I didn't want the summer to end. Although I had just graduated from high school, and was glad of it, the prospect of going to university was completely unappetizing. I had poured through the course calendars of various institutions, but I could not find one college or university that offered anything resembling my interests. What I really wanted was to spend a winter working in Banff and skiing with all my new pals. I had tentatively lined up a part-time job at the station: two days a week relief in the baggage room and two days janitorial. A winter job in the early '60s was a real plum for a would-be ski bum, as unemployment insurance was yet to be invented.

My grandiose plans for winter crumbled when I announced this decision. Dad was adamant I was going to university. After several heated arguments, I backed off. Dad had always told me that Canadian Pacific as I knew it was not long for this world; that in a few years the passenger trains would disappear and there would be limited career opportunities. Of course, I scoffed at his wisdom that proved prophetic, but he won the day and off I went to the University of Alberta.

It was a total disaster. On day one, my so-called student advisor selected my classes for me and, against my wishes, channelled me into a general science program. Apparently, I had no recourse; the registrar's office in those days was God Almighty. Instead of going to classes, I became an accomplished bridge player and, with an equally adroit partner, made ample pocket money from less proficient bridge players at the student union. Reality finally prevailed, with the end of the year closing fast, and I began to panic. However, Lyle Ford took me under his wing, teaching me how to cram and saving me from flunking out and the resulting humiliation for my folks. With exams and university out of the way, I was impatient to get back to Banff and return to work at the station.

The season literally began with a bang. Our first day of work was the Monday before the queen's birthday. We were having morning coffee with Merle, reviewing work procedures and safety regulations, when we were interrupted by a huge bang and crash as the sliding doors came flying off the track, flung across the baggage room floor. We all rushed out of the office to see the rear end of a Brewster bus filling the doorway. Surveying the damage was a young fellow with a straight face and a strong English accent. "I have arrived with some luggage for you blokes, so I thought I'd better leave it inside in case it rains." All of us, including Merle, were doubled over in hysterics. He had backed the bus up and over the eight-inch wooden curb at the edge of the platform. New on the job, his foot slipped off the brake, pushing the gas pedal to the floor. That was the day we all met "Hutch." Not everyone shared Hutch's sense of humour. Within minutes, Rod Adams, operation manager for Brewster, arrived at the station to survey the damage. Rod seemed to snarl and mumble as much as talk but on the inside was a bit of a teddy bear. But when he was wound up, a grizzly replaced the teddy bear. The top of the bus had been peeled back about six feet and the station roof would require significant repair. On the spot, Rod dismissed Hutch, who, with great aplomb, replied, "I suppose that means you'll want the uniform back?" Once again, we all cracked up and even Rod couldn't hold back a smile. The only good news seemed to be that he had delivered the luggage, completely undamaged, into the middle of the baggage room. Hutch did resurface at the train station a couple of days later, hired by Bill Hoffman, the express agent, as delivery driver. Hutch immediately became a local folk hero, and an instant member of our mob. We were all sad to see him leave for Stanford that September on a soccer scholarship. Like so many other Banff summer friends, he disappeared into the world of life.

But a couple of years later, waiting at a bus stop in Auckland, I would hear a gruff voice behind me say, "Move along mate, no loitering here." There stood Hutch, with a huge grin plastered all over his face. The other folk gawked at the sight; a uniformed cop bear-hugging a backpacker. His soccer scholarship had not been sufficient to support him after a couple of semesters, so he had immigrated to New Zealand. Talking old times, he commented, "Working in the express office was the best job a bloke could ever have. I'll never forget the camaraderie and the friends I made at the station. It was such a happy place to be."

The summer of 1960 also set records at the station. In late July, the largest special tour train in history arrived in Banff. It was the Buffalo News Special, travelling as the second section of the Mountaineer. To lure the best applicants in the full employment boom of the '50s and '60s, many companies, like the newspaper *Buffalo News*, offered perks like in-house travel clubs with attractively priced (sometimes even subsidized) group tours for employee vacations. *Buffalo News* partnered with the Eastman Kodak Company, employing 75,000 workers, so easily filled the special tour train to Banff and the Canadian Rockies.

On arrival, the Special was immediately positioned on Garden Tracks 1 and 2 at the east end of the station. The passengers (and luggage) had disembarked from the train in Field, BC, travelling by Brewster tour buses to Emerald Lake and Takakkaw Falls before beginning a two-night stay at the Chateau Lake Louise. The train was connected to the steam plant for heating and plugged into the electrical outlets as the sleeping car porters and dining car crews remained on board.

The next morning, the Buffalo News tour manager contacted Tom Egan (passenger sales representative), informing him the luggage would begin arriving the following day between 8:00 and 9:00 a.m. and was to be loaded and spaced in the appropriate sleeping cars. All luggage was tagged with names, car number and section, roomette or compartment space. Tom then called a meeting with the redcaps, informing us to be on board earlier than usual and to commence loading as the bags arrived. This was the largest group CP Rail had ever handled, with over 500 people and 1,200 pieces of luggage. We were apprehensive. We'd never loaded an entire train before.

On departure day, we began loading luggage by 10:00 a.m. and worked nonstop in between the other train arrivals throughout the day. That same day we also handled the luggage for 12 other tour groups departing on the regular section of the Mountaineer. Unsurprisingly, Murphy's Law kicked in; both Canadians were exceptionally busy, and it seemed impossible we'd get all the bags on board. But help was on the way. In the early afternoon, our pal Clark made the mistake of showing up for coffee. He was immediately pressed into service and spent the rest of his day loading bags. It was a scramble, but with only minutes to spare we were done! All the bags were loaded and spaced on board the Buffalo Special, as well as the regular Mountaineer. We were tired, stiff and sore but elated. We had accomplished what had seemed the impossible; not only was the bag count for all tour groups spot on but we'd finished the task prior to the scheduled departure time.

However, the best news came at the end of the day when we pooled and split our tips. It was the biggest day we had ever had. After paying off Clark for his help, Johnny, Jim and I split $749.00 for the day. In 1960, that was an absolute fortune!

Over that summer, I made peace with my folks, suggesting a year off would help me decide my scholastic future and that seemed to sit well with them. Besides, Dad didn't like to see money wasted. By mid-September, our redcap positions wrapped up and Banff began its winter slumber. As Sunshine and Lake Louise had yet to be developed as even regional ski destinations, there was little employment available. I took a job in Edmonton, working for Alberta Highways, while waiting for summer. But in mid-February I was laid off and returned to Banff to wait out the rest of the winter. And what a winter it was, certainly different from my high school winters.

Wayne, Chuck and Tom, all new pals from the summers of '59 and '60, had moved into a leased house with Aussie newcomer Glen Smith, the reservations manager for Brewster. Number 606 Caribou had been the home of Margaret Greenham, a pioneer resident of Banff and schoolteacher from England. She had established a private girls school called the Mountain School for Girls but closed it in 1947 when she retired. Before she moved away,

Mrs. Greenham continued working with community children through her Merry-Go-Round Theatre and tutoring. Without her help, Grade 12 French would have been a definite fail for me.

Greenham's Mountain School for Girls would never be the same. Within months, it acquired a new reputation and was renamed the Caribou Dance Hall. There was more action some nights at the Caribou than anywhere in town. That spring, after increasing complaints, the inhabitants were encouraged to move, and the house was rented out to a traditional family. Party central was no more.

Summer could not come soon enough for me. The summer of 1961 brought new additions to the station crew. The previous winter in Edmonton, I'd met Bob Anderson, a student at U of A in his second year. Bob had contacted his dad in Toronto, who apparently had some influential connections at CP, so he'd been offered the vacant redcap position. (Johnny Stuckert had resigned, deciding to marry his childhood sweetheart, settle down and start a career with the Bank of Montreal.) Our buddy Clark also joined us at the station, taking a position in the baggage room.

All of us were surprised to hear that Fergie, the Canada Customs officer who had been coming to Banff for years, would not be returning that season. We hoped his replacement would be equally friendly and easygoing, since the Canada Customs office was adjacent to the baggage room. In early June, just prior to the resumption of service of the Mountaineer, we received notice that the new officer would arrive the following morning. Merle had us sweeping and cleaning the customs office when a young fellow walked in with a cooler in his arms, asking us if was it too early to have a beer. "By the way," he said, "my name is Don Donaldson, I'm Fergie's replacement."

Don was a different breed of customs officer. Whereas Fergie was nearing retirement, Don was much younger, at the beginning of his career. He was only a couple years older than many of us at the station and joined in socially at every opportunity. Don's 1951 Dodge was pressed into service, bringing "supplies" to the caboose. Down to earth and a natural comedian, everyone liked Don.

In the early summer some unwelcome excitement got everyone's attention. The westbound Canadian had just departed, and all hands were taking a breather, awaiting the arrival of its eastbound counterpart, which happened to be running late. Usually, the arrivals of the Canadians were within minutes of each other. It turned out to be a very fortuitous delay.

Jim Alexander was sitting on a platform bench, chatting with some passengers. I was just inside the baggage room door when I heard him exclaim, "Hey, look, that boxcar is moving!" I ran outside and, sure enough, a lone boxcar was rolling toward the railway crossing. Earlier that afternoon, the boxcar had been positioned in front of the freight shed and apparently the manual hand brake had not been properly set. The Banff yard has a slight downhill slope to the west and away it went. Dusty Miller and the switching crew were having coffee at the newsstand when Jim rushed in and informed them a boxcar had ripped through a switch. By the time the switch engine was in pursuit, the boxcar had torn through the second switch and was on the main line. The incoming Canadian was only minutes away.

We had never seen the switch engine crew respond with such urgency. About half a mile west, they finally caught the boxcar and made the coupling on the fly, a very tricky manoeuvre. With squealing brakes, the switch engine slowed to a stop and then applied full reverse power, pulling the boxcar at top speed back to the station. The switch engine had barely cleared the crossing when the Canadian came around the corner, less than a mile west. It was a scary few minutes and a near miss, terrifying to think what might have happened had the Canadian been on time. The results of a subsequent investigation were never publicly disclosed, but rumours ran rampant when a couple of replacement crew members arrived on the scene.

But 1961 did prove to be a good summer overall. Although we never experienced another Buffalo News Special, the Mountaineer passenger counts bounced back and both the Canadian and the Dominion passenger counts were stable. Through the summer, the hype from the tour escorts was all about Century 21 Exposition, the upcoming Seattle World's Fair. The tour operators were planning increased departures through the Canadian Rockies, using the fair as the hook, so 1962 promised to be a huge year.

But lurking in the background were signs of things to come. The express department had experienced a significant drop in volume across the country as the trucking industry made inroads. Trains 5 and 6 had been cancelled prior to the summer of 1961, with the remaining mail and express cars shifted to the Dominion. But the most ominous development was the announcement in late summer that the Trans-Canada Highway would open from coast to coast in August of 1962. The motorcoach tour operators had been anticipating this announcement for years and were more than ready to enter the marketplace. Unknown to us, however, a sharp decline in passenger rail travel was coming.

And, perhaps in an equally ominous development, I applied and was accepted for a position with the Bank of Montreal, commencing in October. Three friends were already working at the bank, and a bank job seemed to placate parents eager to see their son embark on a career path. However, my motivation for taking the job was highly suspect; I wanted to stay in Banff for the winter and needed an income. I had no intention of staying with the bank past spring and had already made secret arrangements to return to the railway for the 1962 season.

My redcap position finished for the 1961 season in early September, so I had a couple of weeks to burn before my October start with the bank. My pal Wayne had bought a '57 Thunderbird that summer, so it was time for travel – but a road trip not a train trip, and to a different sort of destination: Las Vegas. Since 21 was the age of majority in Nevada, an older friend returning to university gave me his driver's license and birth certificate. Photo ID had yet to appear on the scene.

I thought I was very cool, heading off to Vegas at 18. We took turns behind the wheel and drove straight through. The interstate highway system was yet to be built and Vegas, therefore, a 20-hour journey. Early in the morning, we stopped for breakfast at a roadside diner in a small town called Mesquite. My first stop was the men's room, and in each stall was a slot machine: my first clue that things would be very different on this vacation.

A couple of hours later, we arrived in Vegas and checked into the Stardust. Wayne had been to Vegas before, so he led us boldly through the lobby to begin five days of chaos. As soon as we checked in, we went to the pool. I was stunned to see a poolside bar and bikini-clad cocktail waitresses, an instant reminder that we were not in Canada. It was a sight we'd never seen and immediately ordered a beer. Even at the pool bar, the service level was over the top, friendly and far more attentive than anything ever experienced in Banff. So good that, by the end of the afternoon, a nap was in order.

I woke in early evening to find Wayne's note that he would meet me in the casino. I showered, put on my best duds and walked into the casino to learn my next lesson of the day from the doorman, the largest human being on the planet, in a Stardust blazer. He asked me where I thought I was going: "You need a suit and tie in the casino after 6:00 p.m. If you don't have one, get one, or you won't get into any casino on the strip."

Suits in the menswear store at the Stardust were way beyond my budget, so I found a shop in the Yellow Pages in downtown Vegas that was still open. I gave him my measurements over the phone, and, in what seemed only minutes later, a taxi driver knocked on my door with my $90 suit. "I've delivered lots of food, booze and hookers to rooms before," he said, "but I've never heard of anyone ordering a suit over the phone. Are you nuts?"

The suit fit like a glove and off I went to the casino. The same bouncer met me at the door and said, "Nice suit kid, now let's see your ID." When I brandished my borrowed ID, he rolled his eyes but let me in. Wayne had long since departed for other places. I spotted my afternoon cocktail waitress sitting at the bar, so I put on my best "Lance Romance" approach. She looked at me with a hint of a smile and said, "Terry, we had some fun at the pool this afternoon, but you are way over your head here." The bartender, leaning on the bar taking in the exchange, said, "I've got some advice for you too, kid. When you're in the bar using phony ID, don't use your real name. By the way, nice suit." My face must have been flaming red as I beat a hasty retreat.

Over the next couple of days, my naïveté continued to take the lead and I blew almost half of what it took me all summer to save. I got angry at the world but mostly at myself. Lesson number three was expensive: don't gamble if you can't afford to lose. But, in hindsight, the trip to Vegas was a beginning for me.

The drive back to Banff seemed extra long but gave me lots of time to reflect on Vegas versus Banff. Working at the train station had me living in a bubble – amidst the natural, spectacular beauty of our surroundings – a simpler life with fewer distractions. I wondered if that was Banff's attraction for tourists also. Las Vegas, on the other hand, seemed about food, booze and nonstop entertainment. And money. The realization that tourism had more than one face was new to me.

The money I lost gambling made it a tough winter for me, as the bank paid peanuts. By January, I had spent the rest of my summer savings and station life seemed light years away. But, finally, it was May and the summer of 1962. I was elated to quit the bank and went back to the good old CPR. Life was good again.

A VERY SOCIAL CABOOSE

In the late 1950s and early '60s, tourism had been on the upswing in Banff, creating critical staff housing shortages. The local population had never met the seasonal demands of tourism. Most summer staff came from towns and cities across the country, which meant accommodation would have to be a major requirement of employment. But many businesses chose to pretend the problem didn't exist. Often jobs went begging because prospective workers found no place to live.

CP was far ahead of the loop and never had that problem in Banff. The Banff Springs could accommodate every employee, up to about 900 each summer, and the company also had the resources to meet housing demands of the station staff. In the 1950s, the bunkhouse across from the station was remodelled and enlarged and, once it filled up, cabooses were parked on the Garden Tracks to accommodate any overflow. But two redcaps took the basic accommodation offered by a caboose to the next level.

For the summer of 1962, Bob and Jim were assigned a caboose of their own, parked on Garden Track #4, located at the east end of the station, with a washroom and showers adjacent. Of the three cabooses housing employees, the redcap caboose became the social centre for the station and, on occasion, a home away from home for many of our summer friends.

On Friday, after the departure of the last train of the day, Don Donaldson, our customs officer and often fearless leader, would visit all departments, taking up a collection to buy the beer, filling an iced container that lived in the trunk of his car. He'd back his car up to the caboose and happy hour was on. Happy hour was usually more social than an opportunity for heavy-duty drinking. But, as the season progressed, happy hour continued well into the evening, attracting a crowd, along with guitars and ukuleles tuned.

A regular attendee at the Friday happy hour was Patrick Nolan, the CPR policeman. Pat was a true Irishman and loved to have a beer with the boys but first and foremost was a policeman. Pat was fair but firm. If we stuck with Friday and Saturday nights, the quietest days of the week around the station, and had the mess cleaned up around the caboose before people and trains began to arrive the next morning, all was good. He also turned a blind eye to our occasional forays up to the second floor of the Upper Annex at the Banff Springs, if we kept the noise down and departed the premises by 11:00 p.m. After that, you could be in deep trouble for trespassing. Why the second floor of the Upper Annex? That's where the dining room waitresses lived!

Over the summer of the "Caboose," we began to change our perceptions of the "fairer sex." We all had girlfriends, but a strange new revelation began to seep into the equation. As we began the passage from often raucous, insecure teenagers to young adults, we could become friends, not just lovers. By midsummer, some of our "lady friends" were showing up at the station and the caboose, not as dates or in couples but as individuals and part of the gang. Friendships were budding; this was the watershed summer for "The Boys and Girls from Banff." Many of the group have remained close friends to this day.

WHERE WERE YOU IN '62?

In 1962, as tourism in the Canadian Rockies experienced a banner year, it shared co-star billing with the main event of the decade: the Seattle World's Fair. From opening day, on April 21, the fair was a record-setting success, attracting over ten million visitors before closing on October 21. It was the place to be in 1962. "Be there or be square" went the saying.

Tour operators the world over embraced the fair, and two or three days in Seattle could easily be added to the already popular Canadian Rockies and Vancouver rail-tour itineraries. Travel by rail to the west coast spiked. The Dominion and the Canadian were packed all summer, and the northern-tier railroads from Chicago, including Northern Pacific and Great Northern, jumped on the bandwagon, adding extra capacity. Much of this volume would feed CP Ferries to Victoria and Vancouver and take the train through the Rockies for the return to Chicago. The huge increase in advance bookings by US operators indicated the Soo Dominion would be unable to service the demand during the summer peak. The solution was to bring back the Mountaineer for one more, and as it transpired, final, season.

CP experienced an influx of summer tourists almost a month earlier than the traditional beginning of the summer season. Tour operators eager to cash in on the opening dates of the World's Fair were booking space on Canadian Pacific's Winnipegger from Minneapolis, connecting to the Dominion in Winnipeg. Most itineraries included a night in Banff before Vancouver and, ultimately, Seattle.

Traditionally, redcaps were not brought onto the payroll until the commencement of the Mountaineer in early June, but I visited with Merle in late April and noted how busy the Dominion and the Canadian seemed to be. He was definitely short-staffed and said, "Why don't you ask to see if it would be OK to put on your red cap and work the trains? We can't put you on the payroll yet, but the tips might be worth it." Mr. Newell, the station agent, was in favour, and for the next month I worked for tips, averaging about \$40 per day. As \$1.50 per hour was the going wage back then, I was well ahead of the game. In the first week, I had made more in tips than my monthly salary at the bank. This surge in early season business was a harbinger of things to come.

The summer was a blockbuster. The tour operators were travelling with full departures of 44 to 48 passengers. Canadian tour operators that we'd never seen before, like UTL Holiday Tours and Horizon Holidays from Toronto, and Tourvac from Montreal, suddenly appeared on the scene. From overseas, Hapag Lloyd from Germany, Thomas Cook from the UK and CN Tours from France, to name a few, became regulars on the weekly traffic advisories forwarded by the sleeping and dining car office. Tour groups, mostly the domain of the Mountaineer in past years, were now accommodated by the Canadian and the Dominion, and the consists of both trains had been increased to the maximum. Loading tour groups on these trains became a challenge, as the Canadians and the Dominions had only ten-minute stops.

CN Tours from France was a division of the Paris office of Canadian National Railway, CP's transcontinental competitor. But Canadian National did not operate trains to Banff, the big hook for travel to the Canadian Rockies from Europe. CN

Tours flew to Montreal from Paris, travelled Canadian National to Jasper and motorcoached to Banff, staying at the Mount Royal or the Gammon Motel. We'd receive their luggage from a Brewster baggage bus to be loaded on the evening Dominion for the return to Montreal. On their very first departure, after loading the luggage on board the train, we approached the escort, informing him our handling charge was 20 cents per bag. He responded, "My escort instructions say CP redcaps cannot request payment for loading luggage, so I owe you nothing," and walked away. Minutes prior to train departure, he came running back to the baggage room in a panic, insisting that 34 bags had arrived on the baggage bus: one of his bags was missing. Jim politely responded, "Sir, we only received 33 bags, so perhaps one of the bags is still at the hotel. We'd like to help you, but we have other groups to load that do pay for our services, so you'll have to wait your turn." The loss of a bag puts terror into the heart of any escort, especially when the train is about to leave. Reluctantly, he forked over the amount owing to us as Jim went through the motions of calling the hotel, miraculously recovering the bag as the train was about to depart. We'd actually ditched the bag out of sight in the baggage room, since the redcaps in Field had already warned us that the CN escort had stiffed them. By avoiding payment to the redcaps, he'd pocketed the money himself. The same escort was to return again that summer, but he never tried to stiff the boys from Banff again.

Prior to 1962, travel on the Mountaineer followed definite patterns designed by the tour operators to maximize vacation days as well as create back-to-back itineraries, feeding the trains in both directions, thereby securing better rates from the railways. Most operators planned their departures from the point of origin on Saturdays or Sundays, ending the tours on weekends as well, a week or two later, depending on the itinerary selected. Such departures allowed clients to book an eight- or nine-day vacation, using only five days of paid vacation time. Similarly, a two-week itinerary would only use ten days of vacation time. As a result, Saturdays and Sundays had usually been the slowest arrival days in Banff, as the trains departing Chicago, Minneapolis, Montreal or Toronto on Saturdays or Sundays did not arrive until Monday or Tuesday. Similarly, reverse itineraries travelling eastbound from Vancouver departed Banff on Wednesday or Thursday, arriving home at the city of origin on the weekend. Saturday through Tuesday were our slowest days, but Wednesday through Friday departures bordered on frantic. That all changed in 1962.

The success of the Seattle World's Fair exceeded all projections. Every day in the summer became a peak day. Daily departures were offered by the tour operators to meet demand and rail traffic to Banff in July and August was off the chart. By the end of the season, I had banked enough to book my dream adventure. I could purchase a plane ticket to Honolulu, a week at a hotel on Waikiki Beach, passage on a P&O ship from Honolulu to New Zealand, with $1,700.00 left over.

It seemed ironic to me that the busiest summer ever for the Mountaineer would serve as the final season of operation for this storied two-nation train. Sometime in August, I confided in Tom Egan of my hope to travel overseas that fall and therefore probably would not be back in time to redcap for the next summer season. As a CP executive, Tom was in the know and commented that my timing couldn't be better since rail traffic was going to take a huge hit in 1963. "Without the Mountaineer, your income next season will be greatly diminished," he said. I responded, "The company threatens to cancel the train every year, but they never do." Tom knew better. "The decision has already been made. The Mountaineer is finished, there will be no Soo Line train to Moose Jaw, or anywhere else for that matter. CP is doing everything it can to exit the passenger service." I was stunned. Tom never even asked me to keep the information confidential, as it was soon to go public.

In hindsight, I shouldn't have been surprised, but it was a hard pill to swallow; to think my favourite train would be gone. But, in truth, it made my decision to travel much easier and my exit was timely. I wouldn't have to live through the aftermath. The summer of 1962 had a bittersweet ending.

PART V

An Ending or a Beginning?

MOVING ON

At the beginning of the summer, I had been considering making the break from Banff and put my half-hearted struggle with career decisions on hold. I had done a poor job thus far, both at university and with my less than enthusiastic attempt at a banking career. My lust for travel was increasingly fed by meeting so many interesting people from around the world.

Initially, I toyed with going to Europe, which was the thing to do at that time. Jim and I also talked about driving around the perimeter of the United States in his TR-3, down to California, across the Gulf States to Florida, up the eastern seaboard to Montreal and then back across Canada. But, as a budding young hockey player, Jim chose instead to play junior hockey in New Westminster, where his parents had moved the previous year.

In late spring, I met Dave Brown, a traveller who hailed from New Zealand. He was working at the Timberline Hotel and one day wandered through the station. Over a coffee at the newsstand, we became fast friends, a relationship that has endured for over 50 years. He filled my head with stories of New Zealand, where to go, what to do and gave me addresses of folks I could contact for work or advice. About the same time, I met Stanley and Mrs. Kerr from Whakatane, New Zealand, who stayed in Banff for a week during their overseas experience that would take them around the globe. Stanley was a dairy farmer who had leased his dairy operation to a share milker before they set off to see the world. He gave me a standing offer of a job on his farm. In midsummer, I met yet another Kiwi working as a bellhop at the Cascade Hotel. Alan was from the South Island and invited me to contact his parents, who would know his whereabouts should I ever make it to Christchurch. The Kiwis had captured my interest and, so, in August, I booked my travel arrangements to Auckland.

I rode the Dominion to Vancouver and splurged on a lower berth. Once on the train, I could feel the anticipation building by the hour. I was flying with Canadian Pacific Airlines to Honolulu, and this portion of my journey produced a mix of excitement and fear. I had never flown before. On its Pacific flights, CP flew Bristol Britannias, four-engine turbo props with a cruising speed of 360 mph. Flight time to Honolulu was a long seven hours and 50 minutes then.

I was seated in economy and the flight was only half-full. I had the aisle and window seats to myself, which was probably a good thing for more reasons than comfort. Every change in the engine pitch, every bump or what I perceived to be a strange noise tensed me up like piano wire. Despite my attempt to project the image of the world traveller, the crew immediately identified me as a first-timer. They were attentive and reassuring and, within a couple of hours, I was enjoying the experience. What I remember best was the food. I was offered a choice of appetizer, and then the wine service began. I just kept saying yes, please. The first tray arrived, with a cup of soup, a salad and a selection of breads. Figuring that was the meal, I ordered some more bread. That's when tray number two arrived with the main course, followed by another stewardess offering a selection of vegetables from a silver serving dish. I didn't know until later that CP Air was famous for its "two-tray service" in economy. I now wonder what had been offered in first class.

Recalling that flight today is like visiting another world, when customers were pampered by the airlines and flying was a fun and positive experience. The inflight service was impeccable, and the food was fit for gourmets, all reminiscent of the excellent food service in the CPR dining cars. I boarded the plane in grey flannels, a shirt, tie and blue blazer, and everyone on board was also formally dressed.

On arrival in Honolulu, I was met at the airport by a hotel car. I had booked a week at the Waikiki Biltmore to give me a time cushion until I got my bearings. The Biltmore, long since gone and now the site of the twin towers of the Hyatt Regency on Waikiki, was a mid-priced property, but I was treated royally. At that time, Waikiki Beach ended about 110 yards past the Biltmore and the original International Marketplace had just opened to great fanfare. Like "old" Hawaii and passenger trains, it, too, has disappeared into history.

After three of the best weeks I'd ever experienced, I was reluctant to leave Hawaii. But I had booked and paid passage on the HMS *Canberra*, sailing from Honolulu in mid-November. Fourteen days later, we docked in Auckland, New Zealand. I certainly had moved on from my "Banff the Beautiful" and spent the best part of the next eight years "on the road" to "somewhere." My travel bug, fed by my early Banff encounters, has never abated. I'm a vagabond to this day.

EPILOGUE

The cancellation of the Mountaineer after the 1962 summer season was indeed the beginning of the end for the passenger rail division of the company. For over 75 years, passenger rail service had been the number one revenue producer and focus for Canadian Pacific, carrying Canada's immigrants, tourists, business people and families to every corner of the land. Trains were the lifeblood of every community. On the rails, passenger trains had top priority for passage.

But, by the end of the 1960s, passenger rail service in Canada had all but disappeared. Rail travel had peaked just after the Second World War, when Canada's railways carried over 60 million passengers. The decline, hardly noticeable in the 1950s, became a nosedive in the 1960s. By 1977, the number of rail travellers had dropped to five million.

How did it happen so quickly? Advances in air travel meant by the early '60s Boeing 707s and DC 9s filled the skies. Jet planes not only made air travel much faster but initially far more comfortable and doubled capacity. For the first time, air travel became affordable for the middle class. The three-night, four-day train journey by rail from Montreal or Toronto to Vancouver became a five-hour flight. But the big killer for train travel to Banff was the completion of the Trans-Canada Highway, which opened in August of 1962. On opening day, over 400 Airstream trailer owners travelled in convoy from Banff to Vancouver and 3,000 cars a day used the highway through the national park. By the 1960s, most people could afford a car and the pent-up demand to explore the country on your own exploded. The future of travel had arrived. Mode of travel was no longer part of the experience sought – destination was what it was all about.

In addition, motorcoach operators had patiently waited in the wings for the opening of the Trans-Canada, ushering in the age of the bus tour. Motorcoach travel was less expensive, offering more flexible itineraries and the advantages of exploring the open road. Travel by rail, over a couple of years, experienced the perfect storm.

The railway saw this coming. Commencing in the early '60s, Canadian Pacific began a campaign of submissions to the federal government, requesting to exit the passenger rail service. The submissions to Parliament, backed by detailed profit and loss statements, clearly proved that passenger service was hemorrhaging millions of dollars annually on all routes, including that of the Canadian, which only a few short years before had been the darling of the transportation industry. But few MPs in Parliament were brave enough to support the abandonment of passenger rail service, especially in their own constituencies. Instead, the Parliament of the day pushed through a typically government solution and created a subsidy program to keep passenger service alive. They were flogging a dead horse. The subsidy simply threw more taxpayer money at the same old problem, with the politicians hoping for a different solution. By 1977, the federal government was subsidizing 80 per cent of CP's losses and 100 per cent of government-owned CN's. The subsidy legislation played right into the CPR's hand, as the railway knew from the start that government would never allow abandonment of passenger service in one fell swoop. But until such time that it did, the railway's losses would be covered. Not exactly a bad compromise for the railways.

In February 1966, CP was finally allowed to discontinue the Dominion, leaving the Canadian as the only passenger train on the CP main line. The Dominion did resurface for six months in 1967 as the Expo Limited, operating from Vancouver to Montreal, augmenting the short-term demand created by Montreal's Expo 67. The Expo Limited became the swan song for CP's Tuscan-red, heavyweight cars, never to be used again. In less than five years, rail service to Banff had gone from six trains daily to two.

Dad and Mom took the Expo Limited from Banff to Montreal to attend Expo 67, a nostalgic trip since they had travelled to Montreal and New York by train for their honeymoon in 1922. Dad had correctly predicted the demise of passenger rail service years before, and he knew this was their last chance for one more rail journey across Canada.

In 1968, CP submitted its first petition to the federal government to abandon the Canadian but was refused and the subsidy continued. Finally, on October 29, 1979, CP's remaining passenger rail service and equipment was handed over to VIA Rail Canada, the federal government Crown corporation set up to operate passenger rail services across the country. The company of the "National Dream" that had bound Canada together with passenger rail service since November 1885 had successfully exited from the main condition of its original charter.

The abandonment of passenger service was devastating to smaller communities, none more so than Banff. Because of the passenger trains, the Banff station had been the largest year-round employer. The infrastructure was wiped out, including the reservations department, the ticket office, the summer switch crews, car washers and cleaners, the redcaps, the baggage room attendants, food services personnel and supply personnel. Into the 1960s, over 70 people had worked at the station in the summer months, 40 full-time, year-round. By the late 1960s, with the Canadian the only passenger train still in operation, the station staff had been reduced to less than ten employees.

Even prior to the final abandonment, the company's quest to exit the business eliminated all interest in maintaining the classic stations and the beauty of their surroundings. In 1970, the circle garden in front of the Banff station was removed and Victor Sugg's beautifully constructed rock garden was left to succumb to the elements. Within a season, it was overgrown by weeds and brush. Years of effort and devotion were cavalierly discarded.

The willows at the west end of the station grounds are the only feature of Sugg's talent and toil to survive. The Willow Tracks were removed in the 1970s and the station, with VIA Rail as the only tenant, began a four-decade decline. In the early 2000s, a good question might have been, "When will CP tear it down?"

To this day, it is difficult to comprehend how quickly a thriving transportation industry fell apart. Thousands were left unemployed across Canada as an entire industry became redundant. While the passenger rail industry has advanced itself exponentially since the 1960s, it is unfortunate that the major advances to date have been in Europe and Asia. North America has been slow to sign on. But there are indications Banff may be playing catch up.

In April 2017, a spark was ignited, and the future for rail travel in the Calgary-Banff corridor has never looked better. Banff residents Adam and Jan Waterous, owners of Liricon Capital Ltd., announced their company had purchased the lease for the station and the surrounding Canadian Pacific land. The plans are compelling and visionary, with the rehabilitation of the station and grounds as a major part of the project. Their news made my heart sing. Some exciting details of their proposal include the following:

- The major revitalization project is slated for the train station lands and will be a saviour for the Town of Banff's parking dilemma. The historic train station will become a mass transit hub, including a 500+ stall parking lot located at the east end of the station. The parking lot will be built on the land between the main line and Bighorn and Squirrel streets, extending east to the Cougar Street/Squirrel Street junction.
- The classic rock garden, located on the sandhill overlooking the east end of the station, will be restored, along with the meditation garden set in the trees at the top of the hill.
- The Banff ice house has been saved from demolition and will be a centrepiece of the Railway Heritage District, set along the willows at the west end of the Banff station. Adjoining the ice house, other buildings of historical significance will complete the village concept. The Waterouses are also partners in the mass transit feasibility study to bring back passenger rail service to the Bow River corridor between Calgary, Cochrane, Canmore, Banff and Lake Louise. Municipalities supporting the study, results of which will be released in the fall of 2019, include Calgary, Cochrane, Canmore, Banff and Improvement District 9, the latter of which includes Lake Louise.
- The ultimate goal of the project is the restoration of passenger rail service between Calgary, Banff and Lake Louise.

Jan Waterous summarized their interest and involvement in the project most succinctly: "Banff does not have a people problem; the infrastructure of the town can easily handle the people. Banff has a car problem. Currently, it is a parking and traffic dilemma. Our project, working with our partners, including the Town of Banff and Parks Canada, will help to make Banff pedestrian-friendly. We want to move people, not cars." Adam added, "It is interesting to note that Calgary is the only city in North America without passenger rail service. We hope to see this change in the near future."

Will the next chapter for the Banff station be titled "Back to the Future?" I hope I'll be here when it's written.

ABOUT THE AUTHOR

Terry Gainer's family arrived in Banff in 1948 when his father, Frank Gainer, was transferred there as station agent. From their arrival until 1955, the family lived in the residence atop the station itself. During these years, Terry explored every nook and cranny of the station and the surrounding grounds. From 1957 he worked summer jobs there, initially as a porter in the baggage room and then as a redcap through the summer of 1962, the bonanza year of the Seattle World's Fair and the opening of the Trans-Canada Highway but unfortunately the beginning of the end of train travel to Banff. Largely influenced by his upbringing, Terry has enjoyed a career that has been an amazing fifty-year adventure in tourism. Terry Gainer retired in 2005, but he has stayed involved in the industry as a marketing consultant. He lives in Nelson, British Columbia.